Seeing God's Heart

THE CERTAINTY OF HIS LOVE FOR ME

LYNN E. WIEDMANN

NORTHWESTERN PUBLISHING HOUSE
Milwaukee, Wisconsin

Northwestern Publishing House
N16W23379 Stone Ridge Dr., Waukesha WI 53188-1108
www.nph.net
© 2024 by Northwestern Publishing House
Published 2024
Printed in the United States of America
ISBN 978-0-8100-2959-0
ISBN 978-0-8100-2960-6 (e-book)

24 25 26 27 28 29 30 31 32 33   10 9 8 7 6 5 4 3 2 1

This book is dedicated to my parents:

Rev. Harry N. Wiedmann, who shared God's
loving heart with me so I can share it with you.

Rola H. Wiedmann, RN, who showed God's
loving heart in her life of compassionate service
to the sick and suffering.

Contents

Part 3: God's Heart Is On Display in Baptism and the Lord's Supper

Part 4: God's Heart Is On Display in His Gift of Prayer

Preface

What if You Doubt
That God Loves You?

The day before my confirmation, I asked my father a similar question. I was 14 years old. My father just happened to be my pastor, and he had taught me what Scripture says about God's love in Christ. He had systematically taught me the teachings of Scripture and explained how each brought God's love to me. Now, the day before I was to stand in front of the congregation and confess what I believed, I asked him, "What if there's something I don't believe?"

"What are you having trouble with?" he asked. His reaction was not one of surprise or anger or frustration. It was matter-of-fact, as if this was a question he was expecting. He replied as if my question, and every other question I might have asked, was totally appropriate and perfectly acceptable, because to him it was.

Looking back, I now realize that I had spent my entire life asking him questions. And it was his fault. He had an open-door policy. I usually walked through that door during his busiest times and on his worst days. But in I walked and often stayed for quite some time asking him questions and listening to his answers.

I came to expect that, more often than not, he would respond to my question by asking his own more penetrating question. It's like when I asked to borrow the car for the first time. He reminded me that the family depended on that car and asked if I could use it with that thought in mind. He expected me to think my question through, evaluate what I was asking for, and help him arrive at a decision.

His question "What are you having trouble with?" made me think about how I would express my doubt. It made me quickly review what my parents and Lutheran teachers had taught me. The tone of voice my father used made me think of how all my teachers had reacted to my questions. They never bullied me into believing or became annoyed if I pressed the matter. They protected my questions under an umbrella of love. And this gave me safety to ask whatever I wanted. They loved the truth, and they loved me. They spoke the truth to me in love.

Throughout my 40 years of shepherding God's flock, people have asked me questions. In framing my answers, I tried to imitate my dad and the other teachers I had. Once a teary-eyed young woman asked, "What if I can't believe?" "What is it you can't believe?" I asked. She wasn't referring to some fact recorded in the Bible, nor was she troubled about a false teaching that seemed to make sense to her. Her concern was at the deepest level: "What if I can't believe that God loves me?"

"Well, you have plenty of company," I responded. "Faith is not manufactured. You cannot talk yourself into believing in God's loving heart. But God, who loves the unlovable, made it his business to inspire your trust and build your confidence in him."

He gave his Son to restore peace between himself and the world.

We think about that gift at Christmas. God's gift is very much like the other gifts laying under the tree. "For me?" we ask uncertainly, even though our name is on the tag. Then we open the present and enjoy that gift of love. "Is the gift of your love in Christ really for me?" we ask God. "Yes," God answers, "this gift is for you."

When I was afraid at night, I always went to my father's side of the bed for comfort. (When I was sick, it was my mother's side.) At those uncertain times, he reassured me of God's loving heart and his certain presence: "Jesus is with you."

The purpose of this book is to help you "search the Scriptures," as my father wrote in the front of my first Bible. The words found in the Scriptures "are spirit and they are life" (John 6:63). God's Word, along with Baptism and Holy Communion, gives us grace to overcome our doubts and grow in certainty that God is with us, for us, and in us. It gives us a way to answer anyone who comes to us and asks, "What if there's something I don't believe?" It gives us the certainty we personally need to protect that person's question under an umbrella of love.

This book will help you be certain that God loves you in Christ. You will explore the many ways God reveals his love: in the Scriptures, in Baptism, and in the Lord's Supper. Finally, you'll see how you can pray to the Lord who loves you. ◌

> *You search the Scriptures because you*
> *think you have eternal life in them.*
> *They testify about me!* (John 5:39)

PART 1

God's Heart

Is On Display in
Christ

Luke's Record of God's Love

It almost seems arrogant to claim certainty about anything, and with good reason. We hear reporters fudge the data, misrepresent the facts, and fake the news. Others spin reports to fit their biases and preconceptions. It's easy to understand a person's skepticism about whether something actually happened. It's hard to know if we should take something seriously or not.

Today's world is no different than it was when Jesus and the apostles lived and worked. The contemporary Roman poet Virgil and the Jewish historian Josephus reported history with an obvious bias. Other historians spun their eyewitness news to please their Roman benefactors. St. Paul himself complained that sometimes his name was put on books he didn't write.

The third gospel, written by Paul's traveling companion Luke, addresses any uncertainties Luke's "most excellent" friend Theophilus (a name that means "loved by God") may have had (Luke 1:3). We're not told if Theophilus had any doubts about the story of Jesus. Regardless, Luke addressed the certainty question head-on. He wanted Theophilus to be certain about what he had been taught concerning Jesus. So Luke provided Theophilus with credible, eyewitness testimony. He referred to people others knew, reported facts that could be checked, and documented what they and others had seen and heard. Luke also wrote a second volume recording the growth of the early church and Paul's missionary journeys. At one point Luke joined Paul's missionary team and was then one of the eyewitnesses himself.

I am impressed (and honestly thankful) that a man like Luke took the time to trace the story of Jesus' life from people who had seen and heard him and then painstakingly wrote it down—all for the benefit of a single person. What an act of compassion! Incidentally, as a physician Luke made special note of the mercy and compassion Jesus had for women, widows, orphans, and the sick and needy.

Luke wrote these lengthy books so that Theophilus could be absolutely certain. He wanted Theophilus to be absolutely certain that Jesus gives us access to the loving heart of his Father. Luke wanted him to be absolutely certain that Jesus loves people from every nation. Dear reader, I'm writing these words for the same reason.

It's not difficult to spot journalistic bias in many news stories or the spin in some corporate earnings reports. Everything is too cut-and-dried. It all looks too perfect, too rosy. But it is not difficult to sense the authenticity of Luke's reports. The church he describes is too checkered, too weak, and too frail. His accounts ring true as they show all the spots and stains of sinful people. The Christians recorded there all struggled with sin. They struggled with false teaching. They struggled to grasp what it meant that God had "visited [them] and prepared redemption for his people" (Luke 1:68).

But visit us he did. Ultimately, what leads us to believe in the certainty of Luke's books are the descriptions of Jesus' compassion and forgiveness found in them. They are too beautiful to be made-up, too wonderful to ignore. A large, cheerful crowd was following Jesus; he stopped abruptly for a funeral procession. A widow was burying her only son. Jesus touched the body (making himself ceremonially unclean). He told the woman not to cry and said to her son, "Young man, I say to you, get up!"

(Luke 7:14). I'm overwhelmed as I think of the tears of joy shed by that widow and her son.

Jesus' sympathy and compassion are found on page after page of Luke's gospel. His acts of compassion in the past give us certainty about how he will treat us in the future. It's amazing to think that God suffered along with us and felt what we have felt. It's like the pain in the gut I felt when I saw a person severely burned on over 90 percent of her body. This attracts us to Jesus. And when see Jesus' actions and hear what he said, we see the loving heart of God at work.

Jesus knows you—but not in some "watch it in a YouTube video" kind of way. He knows the gamut of human feelings. He knows poverty. He knows pain. He knows loneliness. He knows hunger and thirst. He knows suffering and persecution. He knows dying. He even knows what it's like to be forsaken by God. Without a doubt, when you think about God, words like *merciful, compassionate, sympathetic,* and *understanding* come to mind.

Luke and all the writers of Scripture want you to know without a doubt that Jesus knows you. The next two chapters give two good examples. Q

> *It seemed good to me also . . . to write an orderly
> account to you, most excellent Theophilus,
> so that you may know the certainty of the
> things you were taught.* (Luke 1:3,4)

2

Just Who Is Jesus?

One time Jesus' family thought he had a mental breakdown due to exhaustion and tried to rescue him from overwork. But their love was misplaced because they didn't realize that Jesus was the all-powerful Messiah who had come to bring his Father's love to the world.

On another occasion, some Jewish religious leaders thought Jesus was demon-possessed. In fact, they thought he was in league with the devil—a co-conspirator against the work of God. He was pure evil and had to be stopped at all costs.

Pontius Pilate, the Roman governor who sentenced Jesus to death at the Jews' request, was right when he concluded that the Jews were merely jealous of Jesus' popularity and impact. He, a non-Jew, knew that Jesus was innocent and sensed that Jesus was more than just a human being.

Among the general population, the answers were much more positive. Some considered Jesus to be another in the long line of human prophets sent by God to keep the people focused on the coming Messiah. Others considered him to be the Prophet promised by Moses: "The LORD your God will raise up for you a prophet like me from among you, from your brother Israelites"

(Deuteronomy 18:15). Others thought he was Elijah. They got that from the book of Malachi, in which Malachi predicted that Elijah would come back to life before the Messiah came. But Elijah had already come. That was John the Baptist.

Some confessed that Jesus was the promised Messiah. But by that time in Jewish history, the name *Messiah* had become the rallying point for political and religious dreams and deceptions. The Messiah would transform the Jewish society into the upright and godly people God expected them to be. The Messiah would be a priest and purify the church's clergy. He would restore real worship and foster the proper use of the sacred things. He would be a king and liberate the Jewish people from the crushing oppression of the Romans. He would save them from poverty. He would put a stop to racial and cultural hatred and even put an end to sickness and death.

This confusing array of opinions created a lot of doubt about Jesus. They distracted the people from the loving heart of God and the real reason why he sent his Son. None of these opinions caught the meaning of the passages on which they were based.

And none of these thoughts could reconcile what seemed to be two opposing views of the Messiah found in the Old Testament: The Messiah would be a king whose rule would extend to the ends of the earth. The Messiah would be a sacrificial lamb who would be "stricken, smitten, and afflicted" and "crushed for the guilt our sins deserved" (Isaiah 53:4,5).

Only those who understood the true problem and what the solution to that problem required can set these passages side by side and make sense out of them. The real problems are sin and death. The only solutions are God's forgiveness and his gift of life. We see both at the cross. There we see God's love in action. There we see the divine Lamb sent by God to die in our place. God raised his Lamb from the dead and established his worldwide kingdom based on Jesus' life and death. He gives us new life in his kingdom, and he delivers us from an existence under the power of hell and Satan.

God's perfect, sacrificial Lamb was God in all his fullness, and he was a human being in all our weakness and mortality. Being truly human, Jesus could pay the penalty God imposed on Adam and Eve: "You will surely die." The Roman spear tells us Jesus certainly died.

What is more, as a true human being, Jesus understands the pain and struggles of living in this defective world. He understands the limitations of human bodies: hunger, thirst, pain, frustration. He understands death. Jesus reflects the loving heart of God as he says to you what no one else can: "I understand. I know your painful temptations. I know the pain of your suffering." He can deal sympathetically with our sins and with the problems sin causes with God and the messes it makes in our lives. Jesus is certainly the friend of sinners.

But Jesus is more. The angel Gabriel told Mary that her son would be called "the Son of God" (Luke 1:35). At Jesus' baptism the Father spoke from the bright, blinding cloud: "This is my Son, whom I love. I am well pleased with him" (Matthew 3:17). At Jesus' transfiguration the Father spoke again: "This is my Son, whom I love" (Matthew 17:5). The centurion at the cross said, "Truly this was the Son of God" (Matthew 27:54). St. Paul in his letter to the Romans tells us that Jesus "was declared to be God's powerful Son by his resurrection from the dead" (Romans 1:4).

We can't miss God's loving heart in this. The Old Testament promised that God would come and save his people. Isaiah tells us that the baby would be called "Immanuel" (Isaiah 7:14), which means "God with us." Only God could live the perfect life we are unable to live. Only God could walk to the place of execution to pay the perfect ransom price to buy us back into the heavenly Father's favor. God daily removes our guilt. God goes to battle against our enemies. God walks by our side.

The phrases "Son of God" and "Son of Man" are used in an interesting (and comforting) way. When the centurion called Jesus the Son of God, Jesus was hanging dead on his cross. When the angel called Jesus the Son of God, Jesus would soon be born as a little human baby. Jesus described himself as the Son of Man, who someday would be "sitting at the right hand of power and coming with the clouds of heaven" (Mark 14:62). But when he said that, he stood on trial being mocked, about to be spit on, whipped, and crucified!

Who is this Jesus? He is the Son of God and the Son of Man. Can anyone miss God's love in sending such a Savior? ⚲

True God, begotten of the Father from eternity,
and also true man, born of the virgin Mary, is my Lord.
(from Luther's Explanation to the Second
Article of the Apostles' Creed)

3

In Love Jesus Became a Human Being

"That's impossible!" We often use that expression for something that is hard—completing math homework, getting children to behave, sometimes making ends meet. But we don't actually mean these things are literally impossible to do. We're merely saying that, humanly speaking, the odds against them happening are pretty high.

But when Jesus comes into the picture, everything changes. He can do what is literally impossible for human beings to do—miracles, wonders, and signs. For example, standing up in a boat is easy but not recommended. Standing up in a boat during a storm is dangerous and hardly recommended. Telling the wind to stop blowing and the seas to stop heaving and have them listen to you—that is truly impossible; it's a miracle! "Who, then, is this, that he commands even the winds and the water, and they obey him?" the disciples asked (Luke 8:25); it was a wonder. Jesus must be the all-powerful Son of God; it was a sign.

We witness miracles throughout Scripture. We see things happen that shouldn't be happening. No human being can create things out of nothing simply by saying, "Let there be."

Seas do not separate and dry up overnight to allow millions of people to walk through. Ax heads do not float (2 Kings 6:6). The dead cannot be raised to life.

And virgins don't have babies.

But the prophet Isaiah said it would happen. In love God would come to live among his people: "Look! The virgin will conceive and give birth to a son and name him Immanuel" (Isaiah 7:14).

One day a messenger from God, the angel Gabriel, told a young woman, a virgin, that God would perform a miracle through her. Mary asked, "How can this be?" We cannot dismiss Mary as some naïve, believe-everything-you-hear kind of person. We certainly can't assume she had no idea how children are conceived and born. People who lived in the agrarian culture of Israel knew a lot more about reproduction than many city people did.

Mary's question shows that she knew that not having a mate made having a baby impossible. This is just how things work! There were many virgin birth stories offered in mythology, but those were myths, and Mary was not buying any of them.

So Mary set the miracle problem before the angel. "How can this be?" This was a very important question—a question many have asked. Luke wants us to reflect on Mary's amazement. She knew she had not been intimate with a man. She didn't know how the angel's prediction could come true. *Am I supposed to quickly marry Joseph?* she might have wondered. For Mary, the problem was insurmountable. It would take a miracle.

But the angel had come to tell her that impossible things were about to happen. As it turned out, the "how" would be easy for Mary. She didn't need to do anything. "The Holy Spirit will come upon you, and the power of the Most High will overshadow you" (Luke 1:35). The Holy Spirit would be the agent of God's miracle. God's power would "overshadow" her, and she would conceive a son.

Then the angel gave Mary a sign, information about another impossible thing that had recently taken place. He told Mary that her cousin Elizabeth, a very old woman, was six months pregnant. If God could do this for a woman whose ability to have children was as good as dead, then he could give Mary the power to have a child.

How blessed was this young Jewish woman from the backwater town of Nazareth! God was with her, and she was highly favored. Indeed, she was the most highly favored woman on earth. God was going to use her to fulfill his promise of saving love. But for God's love to go into effect, the Savior had to be born of a virgin. As we saw in the last chapter, our Savior had to be both God and man. Mary would take care of the human side of her son. But only if God himself overshadowed her could the child in her womb be God himself. Only then could God come to be with us—"Immanuel."

Mary's child would be the God-promised King. The angel said to Mary:

> Listen, you will conceive and give birth to a son, and you are to name him Jesus. He will be great and will be called the Son of the Most High. The Lord God will give him the throne of his father David. He will reign over the house of Jacob forever, and his kingdom will never end. (Luke 1:31-33)

That's a whopper of a promise for a baby!

Here again we get a glimpse into the gracious heart of God. He is willing and able to do the impossible: to love sinners and use them in his good and gracious plans for the world.

God always performs miracles to further the course of his justice and love. There is a silly debate about whether God could create a stone so large he couldn't lift it. But that's not related to his love for us. He has never promised to spend his time creating stones or lifting them. That would accomplish no loving and gracious purpose for the world of people God cares about. He devotes all of his time and energy making all things work together for our good. We don't need a stone that God can't lift. But we need a Father with a loving heart, a Father who gave us his Son to save people.

Mary was given even more proof of God's love for the world. When she walked through the door of her cousin Elizabeth's house, the baby in Elizabeth's womb jumped for joy, and by the Spirit's power Elizabeth recognized that "the mother of [her] Lord" had walked through the door (Luke 1:43). ⌕

Nothing will be impossible for God. (Luke 1:37)

4

Jesus, Where Do You Come From?

My mind is always filled with questions. Many of them have to do with the Bible. In this chapter we'll focus on a question the people in Jesus' day had about him: Where did Jesus come from?

The Bible reports that the crowds, the Pharisees, the temple guards, and others asked Jesus, "Where do you come from?" In Scripture we find a confusing array of answers. Some answers came from people who hated Jesus and tried to kill him. Others came from people who misunderstood the role of the Messiah in God's plan of salvation and hopelessly misunderstood Jesus' mission. But another answer came from those who took note of the wonderful words Jesus spoke and the merciful miracles he did.

So where did Jesus come from?

What's interesting is that everything Scripture says about Jesus' place of origin relates to the love God has for you and me. So let's explore that; we'll start with Nazareth.

The gospel writers wanted to make it clear that Jesus came from the Galilean town of Nazareth. In fact, the phrase "Jesus of Nazareth" appears 18 times in the gospels and the book of Acts. Even Pontius Pilate identified Jesus like that on the sign he fastened over Jesus' head on the cross.

Nazareth was not a very popular place. When one of Jesus' future disciples, Nathanael, heard that Jesus came from there, he replied, "Nazareth! Can anything good come from there?" (John 1:46). Of course, Nathanael would soon find the answer to his question.

Jesus grew up in Nazareth and would carry out much of his ministry in the nearby town of Capernaum. The prophet Isaiah talks about the blessings the people in this area would someday receive when the Messiah arrived: "In former times, he humbled the land of Zebulun and the land of Naphtali, but in the latter time he will cause it to be glorious. . . . The people walking in darkness have seen a great light. For those living in the land of the shadow of death, the light has dawned" (Isaiah 9:1,2).

The gospel writer Matthew helps us understand that God's heart was beating in love for us when he had his Son grow up in Nazareth. Matthew wrote, "He settled in a city called Nazareth. So what was spoken through the prophets was fulfilled: 'He will be called a Nazarene'" (Matthew 2:23). You would think the Messiah would be raised in the capital city of Jerusalem. But no, he was raised in the humble, little town of Nazareth as the child of a young woman and her carpenter husband. All of this makes the point that Jesus was a humble man who came to save humble sinners like you and me.

But Jesus was actually born in Bethlehem. So Jesus was from there too. A census law imposed by the leader of the Roman Empire, Caesar Augustus, required that everyone in the Roman Empire go to their hometowns to register for taxation purposes. The ancestors of Jesus' father, Joseph, came from Bethlehem. So that's where Mary and Joseph went to fulfill their obligation to the government.

Bethlehem was a small town like Nazareth. But unlike Nazareth, Bethlehem was a place from which good things came. It was famous as the home of Israel's greatest king, King David.

The Savior would be humble, of course. But he would also be the greatest King ever born, sitting forever on King David's throne, ruling over all things for the sake of his church.

This combination shows God's love in action. The Savior would be humble to save us, and he would be a great King who would rule over all things for his people and establish a heavenly kingdom where his people would live forever in peace.

There is yet another answer to the question "Jesus, where do you come from?" One time Jesus fed five thousand men and their families with five small loaves of bread and two small fish. Most of the people there saw Jesus as a manager of a perpetual cafeteria or a goose that would lay golden eggs. Such people didn't really care where Jesus came from, just that they would have access to his power.

After Jesus performed this miracle, in love he wanted to steer the people toward the truth about himself. He wanted them to understand that he was not merely a great man but the Son of God come to live among them, release them from Satan's grasp, and satisfy their greatest need! He told them, "The bread of God is the one who comes down from heaven and gives life to the world. I am the Bread of Life" (John 6:33,35).

Yet in spite of Jesus' miracle and his explanation of where he came from, many among his followers found his words too hard to grasp. So they left. But by God's grace, some continued to follow him.

You have remained by Jesus' side. You believe the truth that Jesus humbled himself for you, came down from heaven as your Immanuel, and rose again as your Savior-King. How much God loves you! Q

*The bread of God is the one who comes down
from heaven and gives life to the world.
I am the Bread of Life.* (John 6:33,35)

5

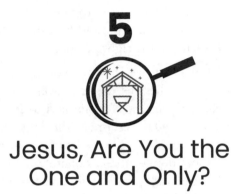

Jesus, Are You the One and Only?

Can you be sure that Jesus *is* the Savior of the world? Can you claim that Jesus is the *only* Savior of the world?

If you're asking those questions, you're not alone. The gospel writer Matthew relates the account of another Christian, John the Baptist, who was also asking questions. An imprisoned John the Baptist sent some of his disciples to ask Jesus, "Are you the Coming One or should we wait for someone else?" (Matthew 11:3).

But John publicly announced that Jesus was the coming Savior. He announced him as the Lamb of God. His death would be God's sacrifice for the sin of the world. Why did John have doubts?

We shouldn't be too hard on John. After all, his short ministry ended when he rebuked King Herod, who, among any number of other sins, was committing adultery with his brother's wife. Now John was in prison. And where was Jesus? Why wasn't he helping his friend? Maybe he couldn't help John. Jesus was not meeting his expectations. Perhaps John had been mistaken about Jesus. In a moment of weakness, he doubted.

But notice the nature of John's doubt. John did not doubt God's love. He knew God would fulfill his promise of a Savior. He just didn't know if Jesus was it. But John did the right thing. He went to Jesus for the answer. He trusted Jesus' honesty and love, even if Jesus might not have been the Messiah. John knew that Jesus would take him to the loving heart of God, who had either sent the Messiah or would send him in the future. John wanted to put his trust in the right person, that's all.

Jesus gave John the answer he was looking for. He offered John visible proof that he was the true Messiah. "Go, report to John what you hear and see," Jesus said to John's disciples (Matthew 11:4). In the Old Testament the prophets had foretold that the Savior would display the loving heart of God, and that's what Jesus was doing in very concrete ways. "The blind receive sight, the lame walk, those who have leprosy are cured, the deaf hear, the dead are raised, and the gospel is preached to the poor" (Matthew 11:5). Astounding miracles! But even more, they were signs that proved that the one who did them was the Messiah. And as the Messiah, Jesus was using his power for the good of the people around him with love that no one else had ever shown.

Jesus offers us the same proof that he is God's promised Savior. Everything he said and did matched perfectly with the predictions of the Old Testament prophets. These prophets described the coming Savior in specific terms, and Jesus was doing exactly what they had predicted the Savior would do. With this proof, the loving heart of Jesus protected John and the rest of the people from false Messiahs.

If all else fails, look at the miracles. Jesus once healed a man born blind. When the religious leaders asked the man about Jesus, he testified, "He is a prophet" (John 9:17). When they challenged him on that, he stated the obvious, "That's amazing! . . . You do not know where he comes from, yet he opened my eyes. We know that God does not listen to sinners. But he does listen to anyone who worships God and does his will. From the beginning of time, no one has ever heard of anyone opening the eyes of someone born blind. If this man were not from God, he could do nothing" (John 9:30-33).

The leaders had prejudged Jesus and anyone who believed in him. Without proof yet with absolute certainty, they claimed that Jesus was a fraud. Their claim of uncertainty was merely a cover-up for the absolute certainty of unbelief. They would have nothing to do with Jesus no matter how many miracles he performed! How blind!

John's world was filled with rot and decay. Arrogant and wicked people, both from the Jewish nation and its Roman conquerors, boldly resisted God and lived in defiance against his will. "God can't tell us what to do, and he can't stop us from doing what we want."

John expected Jesus to do something about this. In fact, God had told John to predict that Jesus would overthrow evil people and God's enemies: "His winnowing shovel is in his hand, and he will thoroughly clean out his threshing floor. He will gather his wheat into the barn, but he will burn up the chaff with unquenchable fire" (Matthew 3:12). John's prophecy was right, but he did not realize that the prophecy would be fulfilled long after he died.

I once had the opportunity to counsel a young girl during a devastating time in her life. The 12-year-old looked me right in the eye. Her look betrayed a mix of anger and pain. God could have saved her best friend from death. She expected nothing less from the Lord in whom she believed, but he did nothing to help. I urged her to go lay her doubt at Jesus' feet and ask him if he really is the One.

I reminded her of this story. Jesus didn't rebuke John or his disciples. He did not resent John's doubt or answer him harshly. He simply pointed to everything he was doing in fulfillment of Old Testament prophecy. Nor did Jesus explain to John why he was not rescuing him from prison. Clearly Jesus had sent John to Herod to rebuke him. Herod too had a time of grace. John warned him about the judgment to come and urged him to repent. What's more, God clearly had something better in store for John—a short ministry followed by an eternity in the presence of God's love.

Jesus is the One. Don't be afraid of putting all your eggs in one basket. Put your life and eternity in his hands. ✑

I give them eternal life, and they will never perish.
No one will snatch them out of my hand. (John 10:28)

6

The Bottom Line: God's Love Versus Our Sin

How do people deal with sin? The list is long, and in your experience—with yourself and with others—you can likely add to it.

Some people believe that deep down inside they are not really that bad. They are sure God loves them just the way they are. They find other people who are quite a bit worse than they are and conclude that they're safe being in the upper 50 percent.

Some people try to keep their nose clean and conclude that God can't expect more than that. They consider themselves regular joes. They try their best. They do what's expected of them. They are not a drain on society.

Other people play the religion game and conclude that if they're members of a church or religious organization, they are spiritual and that's all that God requires. They are thrilled when a really bad sinner repents and gives his or her life to Jesus. They are sure that there is a special place in heaven for these poor souls.

But some people are just the opposite. They are plagued by a single sin that haunts them day and night—the kind of sin for which they cannot forgive themselves. They conclude that God, in his heart of hearts, feels the same way.

On an even sadder level, some people look back on their lives and see an unending train wreck of bad behavior, destroyed relationships, and godless living. I once asked a man if he thought he was going to heaven or hell. Without a moment's hesitation he said, "I'm going straight to hell!" I had to ask him if he really wanted to go there. No matter what this person may have said, however, he didn't really mean it. He really didn't want to say, "I deserve to be punished by God during this life and abandoned by God forever in the torments of hell." Deep down inside he was looking for hope. Perhaps he could change. Perhaps he could make up for the wrong he'd done.

The human heart has a hard time dealing with sin. Let's contrast that with the heart of God.

God's heart is filled with kindness, mercy, and grace. Don't get me wrong—there will be a day of reckoning when everyone who dies in sin will be judged and sentenced. But God is putting that day off. Peter explained why: "He is patient for your sakes, not wanting anyone to perish, but all to come to repentance" (2 Peter 3:9). Paul said the same: God our Savior "wants all people to be saved and to come to the knowledge of the truth" (1 Timothy 2:4).

Some religious leaders once asked Jesus why he was associating with sinful people like tax collectors and prostitutes. Jesus gave them their answer in three parables: the lost sheep, the lost coin, and the prodigal son.

I would argue that these three parables are misnamed. In the first parable, a sheep got lost from the fold. When the shepherd realized this, he risked everything to find the sheep. When he got home that night, he told his friends what happened and they rejoiced that he had found the lost sheep. "The Lost Sheep" is a good title for this parable, but can you think of a better one?

The second parable is about a woman's coin that went missing. The woman searched high and low for that coin. She swept every corner of her house. She didn't quit until she found it. In her joy she told her friends and they shared her joy. "The Lost Coin" is a good title for this parable, but can you think of a better one?

In the third parable Jesus described a father who had two sons. Neither son had the loving and tender heart the father had. The older son kept his nose to the grindstone. He expected that someday his father would give him a special reward for his years of faithful labor. The other son was worthless. He was of no value to the farm and couldn't have cared less about working to support his aging father. He was only interested in getting away from all that responsibility. To fund his escape, he asked for his inheritance money. The first chance he got, he took the money and left.

In time, poverty and famine drove the younger son to his senses. He returned home, sorry for what he had done and willing to take the consequences. Back home, the father had been constantly watching and praying that his son would return. When the son got to the door and blurted out his apology, his father seemed to ignore his repentant heart. The father had only one thought in mind, which he broadcasted to everyone in his household: "Let us eat and celebrate, because this son of mine was dead and is alive again. He was lost and is found" (Luke 15:23,24). "The Prodigal Son" is a good title for this parable, but can you think of a better one?

The religious leaders had asked Jesus why he associated with sinful people like tax collectors. His answer? Because they are lost, just as you are. "That's why I'm here. I've come to find the lost and restore them to my Father."

So let's rename the parables. How about "The Caring Shepherd," "The Persistent Woman," and "The Loving Father"? You may already know your Savior's love. You might live in it every day of your life. But some people around you are lost. Don't be afraid to confront the hopeless ways they try to excuse their sins. Then be bold enough to ask them, "Is your sin really too big for God to forgive? Have you ruined your life or the lives of others so completely that he has stopped looking for you? If you go to him, are you afraid he will shut the door on you?" Then assure them, "If you're lost in guilt, you're just the person God wants." Proclaim to these people the full and free forgiveness that the loving heart of God has given them in Christ. If they believe you, then rejoice along with the angels in heaven. ❑

Forgive us our sins, as we also forgive everyone
who sins against us. (Luke 11:4)

PART 2

God's Heart

Is On Display in
Scripture

7

God's Love Is Revealed in the Old Testament

Have you read the entire Old Testament? If you have, you know what's in it and you have been blessed beyond measure.

But perhaps you started to read the Old Testament and got bogged down. Or perhaps you are new to Christianity and are focusing on the New Testament. When you look at the Old Testament, you might get a little frightened by how big it is. If so, this chapter is for you. In this chapter I hope to show that the love God reveals in the New Testament is at the heart of everything he did as recorded in the Old Testament.

Let's take a walk together through the Old Testament.

The very first chapter of the Bible describes how the world began. It tells us that God created the world in six 24-hour days. Of course, many reject this in favor of the theory of evolution. Even among Christians, many try to combine Scripture's record of creation with evolution. But the true God is not a God of competition, suffering, and death, which is what evolution requires. Rather, he is a powerful God who uses his power in service of his love. In six days he created a perfect world in which there was no suffering or death, a place where he could live with humankind in perfect harmony in a special place called the Garden of Eden.

Humankind fell into sin, but God immediately promised a Savior. Because people were sinful, God had to deal with them differently. He brought death into the world so believers could leave this world and be with him in a new heaven and earth. He punished humankind for sin, first with a worldwide flood and then by forcing people to speak different languages so they couldn't cooperate in doing evil. Even this was motivated by God's love, to keep sin somewhat in check.

In love, he created a special nation from which the Savior would come. He protected that nation. One of that nation's great men, Joseph, was sold by his brothers into Egypt as a slave. As it turned out, God used that evil for good. He put Joseph in a position where he could save his family and many more people from starvation. In the process, Joseph brought his family to Egypt to live with him. There, unmolested by the people around them, the nation of Israel grew large and prospered. As Joseph confessed to his brothers, "You meant evil against me, but God meant it for good, to bring this to pass and to keep many people alive, as it is this day" (Genesis 50:20).

God did destroy the people of Canaan to the north by giving their land to his people and instructing his people to wipe them out. An act of cruelty? No, a well-deserved judgment on the Canaanites' debauchery and horrible idolatry. But God's heart was filled with love for the Canaanites, and in mercy he waited over four hundred years for them to repent before bringing his judgment on them.

God gave his people, the Israelites, many laws, and reading them can be a major hurdle to getting through the Old Testament. But embedded in those laws were pictures of the promised Savior. For example, his people had to keep the Passover Festival. That was a law. But every time they fulfilled that law, they were reminded of God's love in delivering them from slavery in Egypt. And they were reminded that someday he would provide a Lamb, his own Son, through whom he would save the world.

The Old Testament has lists of people whose names you might not be able to pronounce. But those lists remind us of God's faithfulness in keeping the line of the Savior intact—from Adam and Eve down to Jesus' mother, Mary. And those names remind us of God's love in another way: he knows each of us by name.

The Old Testament lists many cities most of us have never visited. By including those places in his Word, God is telling us that he is not in some far-off corner of the galaxy. He is with us here and now. He knows the cities we live in. He even knows your address.

Much of the Old Testament is written in Hebrew poetry. Reading poetry takes much more time and thought than reading history. That's the nature of poetry, but poetry is a wonderful tool to express emotions: "The LORD is my shepherd. I lack nothing" (Psalm 23:1).

The Old Testament helps us remember important ideas by repeating them: "God saw that the light was good" (Genesis 1:4); "God saw that it was good" (Genesis 1:10); "God saw that it was good" (Genesis 1:12); and when he was finished, "God saw everything that he had made, and indeed, it was very good" (Genesis 1:31). Or think of the phrase that's repeated often in the psalms: "Give thanks to the LORD, for he is good. For his mercy endures forever."

What is the Old Testament about?

It is a historical demonstration that God's mercy lasts forever. God told his people through the prophet Isaiah, "In a flood of anger I hid my face from you for a moment, but in everlasting mercy I will have compassion on you, says your Redeemer, the LORD" (Isaiah 54:8). God's anger and judgment over sin never canceled out his mercy and grace.

Moses, the leader of God's people, once requested to see God's glory. Moses learned that God's glory was his goodness. Here's how God described himself:

The LORD, the LORD, the compassionate and gracious God, slow to anger, and overflowing with mercy and truth, maintaining mercy for thousands, forgiving guilt and rebellion and sin. He will by no means clear the guilty. He calls their children and their children's children to account for the guilt of the fathers, even to the third and the fourth generation. (Exodus 34:6,7)

Every time the word LORD occurs in the Old Testament, the writer is always referring back to this passage! Whenever you read the phrase "the LORD," pause in wonder and consider the sermon that phrase is preaching.

God has compassion for us in our weaknesses, hardships, and needs. He responds with acts of grace. This word emphasizes that God is *not required* to act. He acts *by his own will*. And when he acts, he acts consistently with his nature, and his nature is love.

God is "slow to anger." The people of Israel rebelled against God so often, but God continued to forgive them and turn from the destruction he had promised them. When you read the Old Testament, you will spend much time in the prophets. You will hear God warn his people to give up their rebellion and sin, or he would destroy them. Yet how often he set aside his anger and forgave them.

God abounds in love and faithfulness. The Old Testament sometimes uses the picture of marriage to help us understand this concept. Marriage is built on the promise "I love you. I am not leaving you. I will remain faithful to you." Even if people forsake the Lord, he will remain faithful to them. He continues to forgive the rebellion and wickedness of those who confess their sins and return to their loving husband.

Our faithful God maintains "mercy for thousands, forgiving guilt and rebellion and sin." As you read the prophets, you will run across beautiful promises of a Savior. Some are tucked away here and there. Others are impossible to miss, like Isaiah chapter 53, which foretells the Savior who suffered and died for the sin of the world.

The rest of the sermon describes what will happen to those who ignore or despise God's loving heart. He will not leave the guilty unpunished. We are troubled by the anger and judgment of God. But consider: God is angry with sin and plans to judge it, so in love God tells us what he will do if we continue in sin. We take that warning to heart and flee to his love.

Any promise made by someone who doesn't have the power or doesn't live long enough to keep it is worthless. But the One who made promises to his Old Testament people and makes promises to us today is both all-powerful and immortal.

The Old Testament invites you to be certain about God's love. That's what the Old Testament is all about. Read the books of the Old Testament and you will say along with the Old Testament believers:

Give thanks to the LORD, for he is good.
For his mercy endures forever. (Psalm 136:1)

8

God's Love Is Revealed to Adam and Eve

Does God love me? If so, how can I be sure of it?

Good questions.

Adam and Eve stood outside the garden. They saw angels and a flashing sword with the power to attack anyone who tried to enter. Did God still love them?

They had sinned. The snake in the garden planted into the mind of the woman the idea that God had cheated them: "God planted a garden for you to live in, but you aren't allowed to eat whatever you want? God doesn't really love you as much as he claims. He is certainly not as good as he makes himself out to be. In fact, God is a liar. He knows something that he doesn't want you to know. But if you eat of this tree, you'll find out what he's hiding. And you will be like him, which is what he doesn't want."

Once Adam and Eve fell into sin, they ran and hid from God. Run, avoid, excuse, lie your way out of it—punishment is certain!

God came looking for Adam and Eve in the garden. But it was not like a police dragnet searching for criminals; it was a loving Father searching for his very, very lost children. He found them. He punished the one who had deceived them. And then he promised Eve that the Savior would come from one of her descendants. One of her offspring would crush Satan's head. This offspring would end the reign of death and bring the blessing of eternal life to all who would trust in him. Hostility would be restored to where it belonged—between humankind and Satan. Peace would be restored to where it belonged—between humankind and God:

I will put hostility between you and the woman,
and between your seed and her seed.
He will crush your head,
and you will crush his heel. (Genesis 3:15)

With this promise, the question we started with is answered.

Adam and Eve had been dead in sin and destined for eternal death in hell. But God restored spiritual life to them through this promise. Adam and Eve would die physically, but they would not die eternally.

The frightening question that robs us of certainty about God's loving heart has been answered. The guilt of our sin, Satan's weapon against us, has been torn from his hands. With that, the door to God's love opened to us.

God cut Adam and Eve off from the blessing of the tree of life, but his loving heart was at work in that too. He did not want them to live *forever* in sin and misery. He wanted Adam and Eve to yearn for the garden to be restored. And he wanted them to yearn for the day when they would be restored to perfection so they could enjoy the garden once more.

Until that day, God continues to bless us in this world that will someday pass away. Adam and Eve's children were farmers and herders. A few generations later their descendants worked with metals like bronze and iron, made musical instruments, and built cities. We also enjoy the blessings of creativity, music, and making things for others to use.

And consider God's love for the woman, the very one who accepted Satan's lies. What an important role Eve played in restoring life to all people! Adam honored her with a new name that described her role. In what may have been one of the greatest Mother's Day gifts ever given, "the man named his wife Eve because she would be the mother of all the living" (Genesis 3:20). Adam named his wife Eve, *chavah* in Hebrew. Her name is the Hebrew word meaning "life"! This is an unbelievably wonderful name! Eve would continue to bear children and give them physical life. One of her offspring would bear the Savior who would reconcile God to all people.

What a wonderful role Eve played in the history of God's love for fallen humankind—as one of his creations who was now sinful like all of us! And what a wonderful example of God's love for fallen humankind! Scripture traces the line of the women who shared in Eve's blessed role: Sarah, Rebekah, Leah, Rahab, Tamar, Bathsheba, and others. They all join Jesus' mother, Mary, in confessing:

> *My soul proclaims the greatness of the Lord,*
> *because he has looked with favor on the*
> *humble state of his servant.*
> *Surely, from now on all generations will*
> *call me blessed.* (Luke 1:46,48)

9

God's Heart Is Revealed to Abraham

"I'll do that; I swear to God!" The sentence "I'll do it" does not automatically create certainty. But if you add an oath to it, the promise seems to carry more weight. And if you call a curse down on yourself in the process—"Cross my heart and hope to die"—then it seems to carry even more weight.

But when it comes to human promises, nothing actually guarantees that the promise will be fulfilled. Often the witness of God and the dire result of the curse are forgotten. Human oaths get the reputation of being worthless, which is so often the case.

Based on our experience with human beings, we might not be impressed when God makes a promise and adds an oath to it. We have had no experience with someone who *always* keeps or *can* always keep his word. I think about all of the loving mothers and fathers who promise that they will always be there for their children. The promise comes from loving hearts that care deeply for the children, even more than life itself. But no one can keep this promise as stated. We cannot always be there when our children walk out the door for school or work. We certainly cannot keep that promise when we are on the other side of the grave.

But God is different. When God promises something, there is no possibility that he will not do what he has promised. And regarding his promise of a Savior, he goes one step further so we are absolutely certain of his love for us. He adds an oath, "I swear by myself—since there is no one greater than me—that I will give you my love." His oath makes his promise absolutely certain; it is fully guaranteed to be fulfilled.

One of the great foundational promises of the Bible is found in Genesis chapter 12. The promise was made to Abraham. When he was 75 years old, God appeared to Abraham and promised that he would become a great nation, that he would be a blessing to others, that his descendants would inherit the land of Canaan, and that all the people of the world would be blessed through him. In his promise, God revealed his love for Abraham and all humankind because from him would come God's greatest blessing of all, the blessing of a Savior.

But the older Abraham got, the harder it got to believe these promises. He complained to God, "Look, you have given me no offspring, so a servant born in my house will be my heir" (Genesis 15:3). How can you make me into a great nation if I don't have a son? How can I be sure that you will give me the land from the river of Egypt to the Euphrates River, for I will someday die with no one to inherit the promise?

So God entered into a binding contract with Abraham. God became the party of the first part and Abraham the party of the second part. If this had happened today, God might have used the services of a lawyer. He would have had papers drawn up with precise language that clearly stated what he would do and what Abraham would have to do. He would also stipulate the penalties if either he or Abraham failed to complete the full terms of the agreement.

But in the world of Abraham—in Canaan around 2000 B.C.— two people signing a contract would kill a bull and a ram and divide their carcasses in two. Then they would kill two doves.

They would line up the carcass halves with a path between them. The party of the first part would walk through, point to the carcasses, and say, "May this happen to me if I do not fulfill the terms of the agreement." The party of the second part would do the same.

God commanded Abraham to round up the animals, cut them in two, and make the path. But as Abraham watched and waited for the ceremony to begin, a smoking fire pot and a flaming torch appeared and passed through the animals all by themselves. Abraham likely anticipated taking part in the covenant ceremony, but when he saw the smoking fire pot and the flaming torch going down the path all alone, he realized that he was being kept out of it. God alone was making the covenant, so his covenant with Abraham was really a promise. "On that day the LORD made a covenant with [Abraham]. He said, 'To your descendants *I have given* this land from the river of Egypt to the great river, the river Euphrates'" (Genesis 15:18, emphasis added).

Not only that, but God also told Abraham exactly how long it would take to fulfill his promise of a land that Abraham's descendants could call their own. That would take over four hundred years. During that time Abraham's descendants would be enslaved and mistreated, but then after they had become a strong nation, they would be released and led into the Promised Land of Canaan. Incidentally, the reason for the delay was another act of love on God's part. In mercy he was waiting for the inhabitants of the land, the Canaanites, to repent of their horrible and inhumane behavior before using his people as his agent of wrath against them.

The Old Testament is filled with records of sinful actions, warnings against sin, and accounts of God's judgment on sin. Sin is dangerous. We see what happened to Adam and Eve when they sinned. We see the effects of sin all around us. Worst of all, sin is an affront to God and deserves eternal punishment in hell. So when God warns us in no uncertain terms against sin and threatens to punish it, it is not an unloving thing to do. The revelation of God's justice and anger over sin is there so we can flee to his heart of love and the Savior. This is the meaning of the Old Testament. God's promise to Abraham is the foundation on which the Old Testament people placed their hope in God. The hope God gives us through the life and death of Jesus Christ is our proof of his abiding love.

So as you read the Old Testament, highlight all the promises you find there—examples of the mercy, grace, kindness, and love of God. Treasure them as your own! ☌

> *[Abraham] believed in the* Lord, *and the* Lord
> *credited it to him as righteousness.* (Genesis 15:6)

10

What Is the New Testament Really About?

"These are written that you may believe that Jesus is the Christ, the Son of God, and that by believing you may have life in his name" (John 20:31). You cannot put it more simply than that. That is what the New Testament is really about.

The New Testament contains 27 books. Four record the life of Jesus. One is about the history of the early church and St. Paul's missionary journeys. The last book gives us a look at what God's people can expect as they live out their earthly lives until Jesus returns. The rest are letters with instruction and encouragement for God's people.

My purpose in this chapter, however, is not to give you details about the makeup of the New Testament. Rather, it is to show you that the New Testament is about the love that God has for you in Christ.

The New Testament reveals the highest and best kind of love there can be. It is love connected with Jesus Christ. And you are an object of this love. When Jesus said, "God so loved the world" (John 3:16), he was talking about you because you are one of the people who live in this world. He does not want you to perish eternally. Instead he wants you to have eternal life with him.

Let's look at several words the New Testament uses to help us see the big picture of God's love for the world.

The word *love* itself is at the top of the list. For example, the apostle John wrote, "This is love: not that we have loved God, but that he loved us and sent his Son to be the atoning sacrifice for our sins" (1 John 4:10).

The original Greek language has a number of words that can be translated with the English word *love*. When Jesus said, "God so loved the world," he used the Greek word *agape*. This word refers to love as a strong, lasting commitment, even toward those who do not accept that love. Such love leads to acts of kindness without a care as to whether the other person is going to respond, appreciate, thank, or return love to the giver. (By the way, that's how God wants us to love others, even our enemies.)

So when Jesus says, "God so loved the world," he is saying a mouthful. God's heart is breaking. He is filled with pain because our sins have estranged us from him. He yearns to restore us to the perfection in which he created us. He yearns to restore his whole creation to what it was before. He holds out his love to all.

The second word *grace* emphasizes the loving heart that desires to bless someone who does not deserve it. For example, Paul told the church leaders at Ephesus that he could leave them without worry because they had God's Word, which is the message of God's grace: "Now I entrust you to God and to the word of his grace, which has power to build you up and to give you an inheritance among all those who are sanctified" (Acts 20:32). Grace is *undeserved* kindness. It refers to all the blessings God gives us in love. Above all, it is based on what Jesus did for us. He paid for sin and reconciled God to a world of sinners.

The third word is *kindness*. In the case of God's love for us, kindness, like grace, is undeserved. The word *kind* describes a loving heart that thinks the best thoughts about another person. For example, Paul reminded Titus of the wretched, sin-filled life all Christians had lived before God brought them to faith: "When the kindness and love of God our Savior toward mankind appeared, he saved us—not by righteous works that we did ourselves, but because of his mercy. He saved us through the washing of rebirth and the renewal by the Holy Spirit" (Titus 3:4,5).

Acts of kindness flow out of God's loving heart. They are words and actions that say and do what is best for people. Of course, what is best for me does not always refer to what I want at the moment. It refers to what is good for me over the long haul. God's definition of *best*, of course, refers to the longest haul of all—what's best for my eternal salvation.

Compassion is related to kindness. It is the pain we feel in the pit of our stomach when we see someone suffering. I remember seeing a young woman with third-degree burns over 90 percent of her body. I could not feel what she was feeling. But I could and did hurt when I saw her suffering. What kindness could I show her? That's always our first reaction. That's God's reaction to us.

Finally, *mercy* is another New Testament word that describes God's love. For example, the father of John the Baptist said that God would send a Savior "to show mercy to our fathers by remembering his holy covenant, the oath which he swore to Abraham our father, to grant deliverance to us from the hand of our enemies, so that we are able to serve him without fear, in holiness and righteousness before him all our days" (Luke 1:72-75).

A merciful heart responds with thoughts, words, and actions that are just what we need—just when we need them. A merciful heart gives love to people who don't deserve it. Mercy always starts with God, not with us. God's mercy prompts our deeds of mercy to others.

You can see that all these words are related. So what is the purpose of God's love, grace, kindness, compassion, and mercy? God has two goals. First, he does not want anyone to perish. The God who created hell for the devil does not want you or me to go there. Second, God wants everyone in the world to have eternal life. I admit that I'm like everyone else who only thinks about what they want for the next five seconds of today and little more. But these two goals are so lofty and long-lasting! In love, God turns my focus to these goals.

The more we understand the mission of God's loving heart, the more we will truly understand the message of the New Testament. The New Testament writers expand our knowledge of God's love by showing God working among us. Jesus walked among the sinners of this world. When we see how he treated them, we understand how love works. It does not tolerate wickedness. But it calls the wicked to turn from their sin, believe in God's forgiveness, and serve one another with God-inspired love.

We hear the sermons of Jesus, recorded for us by Matthew, Mark, Luke, and John. We see his kindness as he shows mercy to the sick. We walk alongside the suffering Savior as he goes to the cross carrying our sin, as he bears our punishment, and as he dies our death. We reflect on his descent into hell where he proclaimed his victory to Satan and those who tragically chose to follow him. We accompany Jesus' followers to the empty tomb where they learned that death no longer has a hold on them. We watch him ascend into heaven to force a wicked world to act on behalf of his church. And as citizens of heaven, we wait eagerly for him to take us to heaven—the ultimate goal of his loving heart.

In love, God has given us new hearts and minds. Jesus has loved us perfectly, and we know how great that feels. Now we are perfectly suited, like satisfied customers, to be ambassadors of Jesus and put God's loving heart on display. We use our spiritual gifts to show others that . . .

- When God loves, he loves the whole world—every son and daughter of Adam and Eve.

- When God loves, he loves for a purpose. He does not want anyone to perish.

- When God loves, he loves all people with the goal that they enjoy eternal life with him.

- When God loves, his love is easy to find. It's in Jesus Christ, his one and only Son.

- When God loves, and until Jesus returns as judge, his message continues to be that "God did not send his Son into the world to condemn the world, but to save the world through him" (John 3:17).

That loving heart of God is what the New Testament is really about. It's about the love given to us and enjoyed by us in Jesus Christ and through faith in him. ✺

These are written that you may believe that Jesus is the Christ, the Son of God, and that by believing you may have life in his name. (John 20:31)

God Reveals His Love
When We Die

Let's think about proverbs for a moment—not the ones found in Scripture but the ones we hear around us. Here are two proverbs that make true but opposite points: "Absence makes the heart grow fonder" and "out of sight, out of mind." I've heard these proverbs quoted since I was a little boy, but they are never quoted side by side because they contradict each other.

Think about another proverb: "Nothing is certain but death and taxes." Is that true? Are both of them inevitable? Some people in the world aren't taxed, and there are people who illegally refuse to pay their taxes. They hide their assets, launder their money, and falsify their returns. So we conclude that taxes are not inevitable.

But what about death? Death is inevitable, isn't it? We see friends, coworkers, sports personalities, and politicians grow old and die. But in the history of the world, has everyone died? We know of two who did not die: Enoch and Elijah. So death is certain in a sense, but if God wishes, he can intervene and make exceptions. And consider what will happen on the Last Day. On that day many people will simply be transported from life on earth to life in heaven.

Can we make a proverb that is absolutely true—one that will admit no exceptions? How about "God's heart as revealed in Scripture is perfectly loving"? That will work. How about this one: "Although death is not certain, life in Christ is 100 percent certain for believers"?

Paul explained to the believers in Thessalonica:

The Lord himself will come down from heaven with a loud command, with the voice of an archangel, and with the trumpet call of God, and the dead in Christ will rise first. Then we who are alive, who are left, will be caught up in the clouds together with them, to meet the Lord in the air. And so we will always be with the Lord. (1 Thessalonians 4:16,17)

Actually, there are a number of absolutely certain things that will happen when Jesus appears on the Last Day. First, "the Lord himself will come down from heaven." Second, "the dead in Christ will rise first." Third, the believers who are alive "will be caught up in the clouds together with them." And fourth, "we will always be with the Lord."

Something else is certain, something that God does not want to happen but will happen to those who reject him. Not just believers will have their bodies and souls joined together again. Unbelievers, who are spiritually dead, will also stand body and soul before Jesus and receive his verdict on their sin and unbelief. "Then he will say to those on his left, 'Depart from me, you who are cursed, into the eternal fire, which is prepared for the Devil and his angels.' And they will go away to eternal punishment, but the righteous to eternal life" (Matthew 25:41,46).

The resurrection is certain for all! Believers and unbelievers will continue to exist forever and ever. There will also be no end to the glorious life of those who are living and reigning with Christ forever and ever in heaven. There will be no end to the miserable existence of those who are suffering the unquenchable fires of hell.

It is absolutely essential that we hold on to Jesus and his gift of righteousness. If we want our friends and family to be truly happy, we will want them to be truly happy forever. The time we spend on earth is too short to matter; the suffering of this life, no matter how severe, is too light to compare to the glory we will enjoy with the Lord in eternity.

Our ultimate certainty is based on this certainty: Christ is risen! He is risen indeed! Hallelujah!

Doubt-filled and uncertain Thomas saw Jesus alive and touched his hands and feet. "Do not continue to doubt, but believe," Jesus told him (John 20:27). Thomas understood the implications of this. "My Lord and my God!" he replied (John 20:28).

St. Paul adds to our certainty with his eyewitness account. He too saw the risen Lord and was personally taught by him. He was able to identify over five hundred people who had seen Jesus alive! It would be possible for his readers to search them out and hear firsthand that they had seen the risen Jesus.

The verdict of "not guilty" on judgment day is another thing of which we can be certain, guaranteed because our judge (who also happens to be our defense attorney) has risen from the dead. This means that our sins have been paid in full. "Death is swallowed up in victory," Paul wrote (1 Corinthians 15:54). No one can take away from us the hope of eternal life. We have and hold it forever because God will enable us to have and hold Jesus forever.

When you are at the bedside of a dying Christian, you can comfort him or her with these words. You can promise him or her something that is absolutely true! For this Christian, everything will turn out well—and forever!

When we leave this world, we will experience the final revelation of God's love to us. Until then we can risk everything, lose everything, suffer everything, and never lose a thing. ☾

In fact Christ has been raised from the dead,
the firstfruits of those who have fallen asleep.
(1 Corinthians 15:20)

12

The Bible Reveals God's Rich Blessings

Would you call David blessed? He spent half his life being chased by his father-in-law, who wanted to kill him. He was constantly at war. One of his wives looked down on him. One of his sons tried to take control of his kingdom. Many of his friends either turned their backs on him or betrayed him. He often faced temptation, and sometimes he yielded to temptation and suffered as a result.

Nevertheless, in Psalm 23 David said that he lacked nothing. Was that true for him? Is that true for us?

In the first part of this psalm, David wants you to think about the tender, loving heart of God. "The LORD is my shepherd" (verse 1). The heart of a shepherd is soft and gentle yet powerful when necessary. The shepherd stays close to his sheep always. The loving shepherd does whatever the sheep need him to do.

The psalm catches God's Swiss-Army-knife ability to provide for all our needs. *"I lack nothing"* (verse 1, emphasis added). You too can say that. That's not because you don't need anything. Nor can you claim to be self-sufficient. Rather, you have a loving

God who has brought you into his fold and keeps you safe there. If you have him, you truly lack nothing.

Because David is connected to his Good Shepherd, he and every believer can say, "He causes me to lie down in green pastures. He leads me beside quiet waters" (verse 2). Like sheep who are led to green pastures where they have all they need; like sheep who are led to quiet waters where they can drink without being swept away by the rushing stream—our Good Shepherd provides everything we need without our needing to worry about where it will come from or how we will get it.

David counts restoration as a blessing. "He restores my soul" (verse 3). Sometimes the shepherd must lead the flock far and wide on treacherous paths to find the pasture he intends to give them. The sheep are exhausted. They are tired, thirsty, and hungry. God does not eliminate trouble or strain from our journey. And when we are worn out, when we are oppressed by those who care little about our physical lives and less about our spiritual lives, God restores our hope and strength. The tenderhearted, loving God knows how much we can bear and how many trials we can endure. He restores us through the promises of Scripture, as we remember our baptism, and as often as we eat at the Lord's Table.

David counts God's guidance as a blessing. "He guides me in paths of righteousness for his name's sake" (verse 3). David calls God's paths "paths of righteousness." Some have other words for them: *restrictive, confining, slavish, out-of-date.* But the sheep are more than happy to entrust themselves to their loving Shepherd. They are confident he will lead them on the right path, the safe path, the path to where God is waiting to bless them. The path of righteousness starts when our Shepherd shows us our sin. It continues when he forgives our sin. It leads to the Spirit's power to understand the height and breadth and depth of God's love. It continues on to a new life of service to him.

All this he does "for his name's sake" (verse 3). Often in this book I have talked about God's loving heart. Love is what he is known for. It's who he is, and it determines what he does. It is his good name. That's why God blesses us. He blesses us not for the sake of our sinful name but for the sake of what he has done for us in Christ, so that he can put his love on display.

David had faced death any number of times. The most well-known of which was the time he faced Goliath, a 9-foot-6-inch giant, whose spear shaft was like a four-by-four. As David walked toward Goliath with only a slingshot and some stones, he saw death staring him in the face. But David counted on God to be with him. His presence provided David with peace and strength. And like all of us, David would face death when the Lord was ready to take him to heaven. He confessed, "Even though I walk through the valley of the shadow of death, I will fear no evil, for you are with me. Your rod and your staff, they comfort me" (verse 4).

David was blessed to die in the Lord and with the Lord. We all watch as our friends and loved ones die. At those times the tender heart of God's love will help us give hope to those who are suffering the loss. Of all the things one might hope for at the point of death, God's presence and comfort are the best.

David wasn't just a shepherd. He was also a king. He was Israel's greatest king, a man after God's own heart. So in the second part of Psalm 23 David described the blessings he received from God's Word using pictures from life in the palace.

"You set a table for me in the presence of my foes" (verse 5). The banquet table is set, every square inch filled with the finest fare. Best of all, the Lord is the one spreading out the feast. David's enemies were looking on, and at that moment they realized that God was on David's side. God has spread out a feast for us too. The Lord is filling our lives with the finest fare. Perhaps our enemies will realize that we are blessed and protected in Christ. Perhaps they will ask us to give a reason for our hope.

"You drench my head with oil" (verse 5). In ancient times, before dinner people would use the finest oils to keep their skin soft and smooth. David was also anointed with oil when God set him apart to be king over Israel. Both pictures show God's favor on David and on us. The oil symbolizes the rich blessings God gives us in life and that, along with David, he has set us apart to rule with him into eternity.

"My cup is overflowing" (verse 5). God continued to pour blessings into David's cup, and it was constantly overflowing. Each of us can say along with David, "I lack nothing."

David confessed, "Surely goodness and mercy will pursue me all the days of my life" (verse 6). David summed up God's blessings with the words *goodness* and *mercy*. Just like God's creation was "very good" (Genesis 1:31), so the Lord created David's life to be good. Why did God do this for David? And why does he do it for us? Because God is merciful in Christ, and he fills his followers with compassion, kindness, sympathy, love, and understanding.

The flow of God's blessings did not end when David died: "I will live in the house of the LORD forever" (verse 6). We lack nothing on earth. We will lack nothing in heaven. In fact, there we will see his blessings more clearly and praise his name with perfect understanding and joy. And we will do that for an eternity.

If we want to see the tender heart of God, we need look no further than Psalm 23. Our Good Shepherd supplies, restores, guides, and comforts us. He fills our lives with honor and blessing. And he gives us victory over our enemies. ○

The LORD is my shepherd. I lack nothing. (Psalm 23:1)

13

God's Heart Is Revealed in Words That Can Be Understood

God wants nothing more than to reveal his love for us.

There are certain things God does not have to reveal. When we look at God's creation, it is only logical to conclude that it was created by God. And it is logical to conclude that the Creator possesses "eternal power" and a "divine nature" (Romans 1:20). What's more, when we look inside ourselves, we find a basic understanding of right and wrong. Along with this is a voice that makes us feel good if we do right and causes us pain when we do wrong. Put it all together and people can only conclude that the Creator will judge them for the sins they commit. No one has to reveal that to us.

But there is something else we must know about God—something we cannot learn by observation and logic, something God must reveal to us. God must reveal his love to us and why we can be certain of his love.

Let's turn to the Bible where God reveals this love. Our conclusion to this chapter will be that not only does God reveal his love in the Bible, but he also reveals his love by giving us a Bible written in words we can understand.

We can read the Bible just like we read any other book. This is not to say that everything in the Bible is easy to understand. But as we grow in our knowledge of what the Bible says, the more the difficult sections open up to us. No guesswork is involved. No speculation is necessary.

God uses language in ways we are used to. Words can have different meanings, so we have to keep in mind the context. We do this all the time. For example: I run, and my dishwasher runs. But if I go to a "running store," you know that I am not going there to buy dishwasher parts. Consider the word *day* as used in Genesis chapters 1 and 2 and in other parts of Scripture. A day can mean the period of light in a 24-hour period, or it can mean the full 24-hour period. Moses used it in both ways (see Genesis 1:5 where is it used with both meanings in the same verse). It is easy to see what the word *day* means in each context.

God chose to write his message at a certain point in history and for a certain group of people. The people to whom the Bible was first written were living in a different culture. In order to understand some sections of Scripture, it helps to know a bit about the cultural context. But it is easy to get carried away with this. Some people stress cultural knowledge so much that without it, they claim, Scripture is a closed book.

But the Bible is not a closed book or even a book that can be understood only if we have a sufficient understanding of the culture in which it was written. Consider the parable of the prodigal son in Luke chapter 15. Knowing some facts about Jewish inheritance rights or that pigs were unclean to the Jews might help us visualize what is happening a bit better. But nothing in the account depends on our understanding these facts.

Or consider the account of Jesus raising Lazarus from the dead in John chapter 11. A knowledge of Jewish burial customs might help us visualize what happened when Lazarus came out of his tomb. But it's not necessary in order to understand what took place that day: Jesus' power over death or the Jewish leaders' hardness of heart in wanting to kill Jesus afterward. The account is clear all by itself.

If there is disagreement about the meaning of a certain section of Scripture, it is not God's fault. Rather, it's the fault of readers who force a meaning out of Scripture that isn't found there. Peter made that point about certain things Paul wrote: "There are some matters that are hard to understand in his letters, which the ignorant and unstable distort, as they also do with the other Scriptures, to their own destruction" (2 Peter 3:16).

Jesus sometimes used a word or an expression to get people to think. One time Jesus was talking to a church leader named Nicodemus. He told Nicodemus, "I tell you the truth, no one can see the kingdom of God unless he is born again" (John 3:3 NIV 1984).

By the end of John chapter 3, Nicodemus knew that the phrase "born again" had a very special meaning that Jesus wanted him to learn. At first, however, Nicodemus had no clue what Jesus was talking about. Jesus was tantalizing Nicodemus and challenging him. He was using words that Nicodemus did not understand to get him to realize that he didn't know everything and to start asking Jesus for answers.

So when you run into sentences and paragraphs that make you say, "What does this mean?" the Holy Spirit has put that question in your head because God wants to answer that question for you. He wants you to search for the answer in his Word. Look at it this way: If you were on a desert island all alone with only your Bible, you would have everything you need to understand it. You could study the easier parts of Scripture to help you understand the more difficult parts. You would have all you need to learn the truth about sin and grace, life and salvation, everything God wants you to believe and do.

That's what God in love has given us. The Bible is a book that, without fail and all by itself, gives us perfect access to God's love in Christ.

The Bible contains different types of literature. Each type plays a role in conveying God's love in working out his plan of salvation. The main types of writing are narrative history, poetry, and prophecy. To that we can add correspondence letters, many of which are found in the New Testament. This is an especially useful type of literature to convey God's love. Let's look at each type.

Narrative history.

The history contained in Scripture has aptly been called "his story," that is, the story of God. When you read Scripture, you do not find answers to all areas of history, even the history of God's people. But what you find is the story of how God in righteousness fulfilled his promise to send a Savior from sin.

Poetry.

The Old Testament is full of poetry. In English poetry we look for rhymes and meters. We expect interesting wordplays, puns, and all kinds of wordsmithing to help convey the writer's content and mood.

Hebrew poetry does the same. God could have restricted himself to prose, like we find in the historical record, but he didn't. He also used poetry. Poetry conveys the writers' feelings so well—feelings of joy, anger, fear, and repentance. Poetry powerfully conveys God's promises and love for us. Think of the beauty of Psalm 23, which we looked at in the last chapter.

Hebrew poetry is not like English poetry. As we mentioned, English poetry often depends on rhymes. Hebrew poetry, on the other hand, depends on the creative use of words and phrases. The poet often uses a variety of ways to say the same thing. In a psalm verse, for example, each line might say the same thing but in a different way:

The wicked will not stand in the judgment,
nor sinners in the assembly of the righteous. (Psalm 1:5)

Or the second and sometimes third lines may build on the previous line:

He causes me to lie down in green pastures.
He leads me beside quiet waters.
He restores my soul. (Psalm 23:2,3)

Or the second line of a verse may contrast with the first:

The LORD approves of the way of the righteous,
but the way of the wicked will perish. (Psalm 1:6)

Knowing this, you can often figure out a difficult line in a verse by using the line before or after it, which might be clearer.

Prophecy.

Prophets had a simple job, really. They needed to say exactly what God told them to say and not leave anything out. Most often the prophets warned the people of Israel against rejecting God. They urged the people to return to the Lord, or God would judge their nation. The prophets needed to speak God's Word whether the people listened to them or not. And most of the time they did not!

Sometimes God announced things that were going to happen in regard to the coming Savior. God revealed that he would be faithful to his gospel promise even if his people were unfaithful to him.

Sometimes God foretold what would happen to the nation of Israel. He did this to show that he was the only true God and to prove that the idols the Israelites often worshiped were powerless. One of my favorite accounts is about Daniel when he was in exile in Babylon. He was reading from the book of the prophet Jeremiah. Jeremiah had written that 70 years would pass between the beginning and end of the Israelites' captivity in Babylon. Daniel counted the years. The time was near, so he started preparing himself and his people to go back home. Two years later, King Cyrus gave the order that allowed the Jews to return to the Promised Land.

Correspondence letters.

God called 13 men to serve as apostles. These men would be the foundation of the Christian church. They would bear witness that Jesus had risen from the dead, and they would write down the teaching that Jesus had revealed to them.

The apostles and the men who had worked with them wrote letters to Christians in various places. The New Testament letters work to preserve the gospel message. When someone attacked God's love in Christ, which is the center of God's being and the driving force of all he does, that person had to be stopped. That was the purpose of several letters. All the letters are filled with instructions, teachings, encouragements, and especially prayers that God would give the readers wisdom and insight into the reason for their hope. The letters reflect the love Jesus has for those he brought to faith and the zeal he has for spreading the message of salvation into the world.

When you read the New Testament letters, explore God's heart of love by watching the apostles endure the loss of everything and do all in their power to share with as many people as possible the message of God's forgiving grace in Christ. ✎

Sanctify them by the truth.
Your word is truth. (John 17:17)

14

God's Word Is Always at Work

Does God's Word work? Jesus used a seed to describe his Word because seeds grow.

The kingdom of God is like this: A man scatters seed on the ground, and while he sleeps and rises, night and day, the seed sprouts and grows, though he does not know how. The ground produces fruit on its own: first the blade, then the head, then the full grain in the head. (Mark 4:26-28)

Isaiah used rain as a picture of God's Word because the rain makes seeds grow.

Just as the rain and the snow come down from the sky and do not return there unless they first water the earth, make it give birth, and cause it to sprout, so that it gives seed to the sower and bread to the eater, in the same way my word that goes out from my mouth will not return to me empty. Rather, it will accomplish whatever I please, and it will succeed in the purpose for which I sent it. (Isaiah 55:10,11)

The message of sin and grace has power. It's this power that brought you from unbelief to faith, from death to life. When Jeremiah was rebuking the false prophets of his day, he spoke of the power of God's Word in contrast to the powerless words the false prophets spoke. He wrote, "Is not my word like a fire? declares the LORD, and like a hammer that breaks a rock in pieces?" (Jeremiah 23:29). God's law has burned away your self-righteousness. God's threat of judgment has crushed your pride.

But God's message of forgiveness in his Word went to work on your heart. Burned and crushed, it made you whole by the message of grace in Christ. Peter impresses on us the power of God's Word:

> You have been born again, not from perishable seed but from imperishable, through the living and enduring word of God. For: All flesh is like grass, and all its glory is like a flower of the field. The grass withers, and the flower falls, but the word of the Lord endures forever. And this is the word that was preached to you. (1 Peter 1:23-25)

St. Paul described for Timothy the work that the God-breathed words in our Bible do:

> From infancy you have known the Holy Scriptures, which are able to make you wise for salvation through faith in Christ Jesus. All Scripture is God breathed and is useful for teaching, for rebuking, for correcting, and for training in righteousness, so that the man of God may be complete, well equipped for every good work. (2 Timothy 3:15-17).

Let's notice the "work" that God's Word does. Most important of all, the Bible has eternal work to do. It teaches us. It makes us "wise for salvation through faith in Christ Jesus." The Bible also has this-world work for us to do. It prepares us for every good work. The Word keeps our eyes fixed on the loving heart of God and his Son Jesus so that we love others and always want to do them good.

Sometimes we need the powerful Word to stop us dead in our tracks. This is the reproof Paul was talking about.

When we go off the rails either in the details of our faith or in how we're living, we need God to redirect and correct us and then let us try again. This is the teaching and correcting Paul was talking about.

Finally, God needs to grow and strengthen our faith in his precious gift of perfection, holiness, and righteousness in Christ. This fills us with thanks and praise and motivates us to serve him more and better. Then he sends us out to work in his kingdom. This is the training in righteousness Paul was talking about.

Paul tells us that we can be sure Scripture is true. God has protected it from the human errors contained in every other piece of literature. It has been breathed out by God into the minds and pens of the Bible writers.

The Word is always at work. Any time you open your Bible and begin to read, the Holy Spirit is working on your heart and mind. In fact, the Word itself is not like the great novel you just finished, contentedly resting in your memory. Rather, the power of God's Word is continually at work within you, reminding you of God's love in Christ and sustaining your faith. This is what Paul was so happy about when he thought about the new believers in Thessalonica. He rejoiced over what God's Word had accomplished in them and what it was still doing in them every day. "When you received God's word, which you heard from us, you did not receive it as the word of men but as the word of God (as it really is), which is now at work in you who believe" (1 Thessalonians 2:13).

What a close connection there is between the work of the Holy Spirit and the work of God's Word in us! The Holy Spirit makes us holy in Christ. So does the Word of God. "Sanctify them by the truth. Your word is truth" (John 17:17). The Holy Spirit makes the kingdom of God grow throughout the world, and he does this through the Word he gave to the church. Paul tells God's people to take up "the sword of the Spirit, which is the word of God" (Ephesians 6:17). The power of God's Spirit leads people to faith. God's Word also leads people to faith.

"Faith comes from hearing the message, and the message comes through the word of Christ" (Romans 10:17).

My wife and I were sitting enjoying our Sunday brunch. My wife struck up a conversation with the lady at the next table. When she found out I was a pastor, I could see the pain of frustration and disappointment—uncertainty too—as she told me, "I don't want to listen to just a man!" After what she had been through, she didn't want to put her hope in the unreliable, uncertain, or downright deceptive words cooked up in the back room of human minds. She was looking for truth. It seemed to help her when I quoted Scripture directly without much comment or explanation. The powerful Word of God was at work.

What love God has revealed to us! We are saved for eternity through the blood Christ shed for us. What love God has shown us by giving us the power of his Spirit and his Word, which has the ability to break through our sinful resistance, bring us from death to life, and keep us focused on the hope we have in Christ. What love he has given us in providing a place to turn to when we are searching for the truth and the presence of God's Spirit. The Spirit is always there, right there in the Word he inspired, ready to go to work when we read or hear it. ⌕

Sanctify them by the truth. Your word is truth.
(John 17:17)

15

God Reveals His Love by Warning Us Not to Reject It

We're going to begin with a couple of doctrinal terms. Don't be put off. We'll go through them together.

Scripture teaches that God's Word is always *efficacious*, but it is not always *effective*. We can count on the Holy Spirit's presence and power in God's Word, always working to lead a person to repentance and faith, always working to lead Christians to a great understanding of the height and breadth of God's love (it's always *efficacious*). But the work of the Holy Spirit can be resisted by sinful human beings (it's not always effective). This is true when the Holy Spirit and the Word tell us to repent of our sins and trust in Jesus' forgiveness.

However, contrast this with God's power at work in creation. At creation, when God spoke his Word, it always produced what God wanted. Nothing stood in its way. Or when God commands kingdoms to rise and fall, that always happens; nothing stands in its way. In these matters, using doctrinal terms, God's Word is always *efficacious* (it is working with irresistible power), and it is always *effective* (what God speaks always happens).

But that's not how it is when God speaks the good news of forgiveness and salvation in Christ. God tells us, "I have paid for the guilt of your sins. I have reconciled you to myself. Believe it, and live in the hope of eternal life!" When God speaks those words, the Spirit is at work with all of his power to convert. But human beings have the power to say, "No, I don't want to believe it." When God tells us, "Read and hear my Word. Grow to better understand my love for you," we have the power to say, "No, I have more pressing matters to attend to."

This is a horrible power we have—to reject God when he tells us to believe or when he urges us to read and learn what Scripture says. God warns us against using this horrible power—a power Satan and our sinful nature always want us to use.

And this warning is a loving thing!

Jesus would soon send his disciples into the world to tell people that the kingdom of God had come. They were to bring the gospel into all the world. Lest they became discouraged, Jesus taught them what people would do with the Word they were preaching. This is important for your pastors who give their full time to shepherding God's flock. And it is important for you as a disciple of Christ when you work with the people in your lives, giving a reason for the hope you have and urging them to share this hope along with you. Should God's people be disappointed when their preaching and teaching and sharing their hope is rejected or not received as warmly as they hoped?

So Jesus told a parable not only to keep us from being disappointed but also—and this is the good part—to assure us that the Word and the Spirit would successfully enable people to know the love of God in Christ and serve him.

Here's Jesus' parable:

Listen carefully to the parable of the sower. When anyone hears the word of the kingdom and does not understand it, the Evil One comes and snatches away what has been sown in his heart. This is the seed that was sown along the path. The seed that was sown on rocky ground is the person who hears the word and immediately receives it with joy, yet he is not deeply rooted and does not endure. When trouble or persecution comes because of the word, he immediately falls away. The seed that was sown among the thorns is the one who hears the word, but the worry of this world and the deceitfulness of wealth choke the word, and it produces no fruit. But the seed that was sown on the good ground is the one who continues to hear and understand the word. Indeed he continues to produce fruit: some a hundred, some sixty, and some thirty times more than was sown. (Matthew 13:18-23)

When Jesus and the apostles would spread the powerful Word of God, some people would resist it. Some would block their ears against it or only pretend to listen. Others would be content with a shallow faith and quickly give it up in the face of persecution. Others would let the worries and cares of the world completely dominate their life. But the powerful Word of God would be successful too. Christians who share the Word with others would experience the joy of seeing people come to know or grow in the freedom they have in Christ.

Don't be discouraged if people reject the Word or fall away. Pray to God that they someday give up their unbelief. But don't let it so discourage you that you give up. Some will believe. Some will take God's Word to heart.

The parable of the sower and the seed teaches us that we too have the horrible power to resist God's Word. God reveals his love to us by warning us against using this power.

God urges us to read and learn his Word, certain that the Spirit is at work there, wanting to reveal more and more of his love in Christ and a deeper understanding of his will for us. He wants us to search for wisdom, knowledge, understanding, and insight into his truth. The Holy Spirit is the Spirit of wisdom, knowledge, understanding, and insight, who uses the words of Scripture, which he inspired, to give us those gifts.

So as we open our Bibles and get ready to read, we pray, "Thank you for the gift of your Spirit, who will lead me to understand your words, trust your words, and use your words to guide me as I journey to heaven."

Jesus knows his people will be surrounded by those who misuse the truth and use their power to stop the truth from spreading. Jesus warned his disciples, "They will hand you over to be persecuted, and they will put you to death. You will be hated by all nations because of my name" (Matthew 24:9). Paul encouraged believers to continue in the faith, and he warned them, "We must go through many troubles on our way to the kingdom of God" (Acts 14:22).

If you're like me, a pain-avoidance specialist, you will do anything to avoid pain. But that can have deadly consequences if applied to our life of faith. Our sinful nature wants to use the boiling sun of painful persecution to make us give up our faith and take the less painful path the world offers.

Unless . . . unless by God's grace we are unwilling to surrender the loving heart of God. In that case, persecution becomes a tool in the hands of a loving God. Pain and trouble, persecution and hatred drive us back to the Bible; they force us to remember and rely on God's promises. They perfect us in perseverance. Throughout its history, the church has expanded geographically, has grown numerically, and has been strengthened spiritually when God used the tool of persecution. Often unbelievers watched Christians say they had hope, and then they found that hope for themselves. Past and present martyrs executed for their faith now enjoy God's love in a far better place than this world.

So we pray, "Lord, thank you for the power of your Word and Spirit that increases and strengthens my hope in Christ. When suffering of any kind comes into my life, use it for your purposes and my eternal good. Help me greet persecution with joy, knowing that in all things you work for my good and the good of believers around me. Help me endure persecution in a way that draws others to you."

Christians also need to guard against the worries associated with increasing wealth. The more a person accumulates what leads to a pleasure-filled life, the more that person starts to worry about losing those things. Wealth may get stolen. Valuables may be ruined or destroyed. Possessions seem to be permanent, but that's deceptive because when people die they can't take their earthly goods with them. Wealth promises so much, but in the end it can lead a person to "gain the whole world and yet forfeit his soul" (Mark 8:36).

So we pray, "Lord, thank you for giving me what I need. Thank you for not giving me too little lest I don't have enough to fulfill my vocation in life. Thank you for not giving me too much lest my possessions draw me away from you. Give me your Spirit through the Word of your grace so I find my greatest treasure in you."

Does the Word work? Always. We can expect many to resist the Word. We confess that we are tempted to do the same. But we know where to go in the midst of weakness and temptation, namely, to the sword of the Spirit, which is God's Word. ⟡

He gave us birth by the word of
truth so that we would be
a kind of firstfruits of his creations. (James 1:18)

PART 3

God's Heart

Is On Display in
Baptism and the
Lord's Supper

16

In Love God Reveals That Baptism Is for You Too

How do you describe yourself in relation to the people of the world around you? You have come to faith in Christ. You are serving the Lord. And so, as a child of God, you are different from those around you.

But it wasn't always so. At one time, all believers were in the same boat as the unbelievers around them. St. Paul reminded the Christians on the island of Crete what they were like before they came to faith. He did this not to drive them into the ground, but so he could strike a contrast between what they once were and what they had now become in Christ.

Paul spoke for all of us, "For at one time we ourselves..." (Titus 3:3). Then he continued with four descriptions that paint a dismal picture of how God found us when he brought us into his family.

We had been "foolish" and "disobedient." We were in open rebellion against the plain and clear laws of God. We were like rebellious children who disregarded their parents and simply did whatever they wanted. The word *foolish* means to know exactly what you are supposed to do and intentionally refuse to do it.

We were "deceived" and "enslaved by many kinds of evil desires and pleasures." The people around us offered us a long life with endless joy and pure pleasure. The greater the offers became, the more they drew us into a trap from which we could not escape. We were enslaved, and the more we pursued the passions and pleasures of the world, the less fulfilling they became. Our appetites escalated, but our joy diminished.

We lived "in malice and jealousy." As we tried to get more and more for ourselves, we were gripped by a mean-spiritedness toward others. They had what we wanted. We stooped to whatever level necessary—cheating, lying, hurting, and harming—to get what we wanted.

And that led to our "being hated and hating one another." We were jealous of the power, position, and prosperity of others. They hated us, and we hated them.

But Paul started his description of the Cretans with these words: "For at one time we ourselves were also" like that. Interestingly, Paul pointed out that the people of Crete were even worse than most. He quoted a Cretan poet, Epimenides, who described his own people like this: "Cretans are always liars, vicious beasts, and lazy gluttons." That's the kind of people the Christians in Crete had been when God found them—vile, lazy, drunken, contentious bullies.

All mission work—teaching and baptizing—depends on people facing the depth of their sin before God found them. And all growth in Christian faith and life depends on people remembering what God did for them when he found them in this deplorable condition. Paul reminded the Cretans about what God had done for them and every believer:

> When the kindness and love of God our Savior toward mankind appeared, he saved us—not by righteous works that we did ourselves, but because of his mercy. He saved us through the washing of rebirth and the renewal by the Holy Spirit, whom he poured out on us abundantly through Jesus Christ our Savior, so that, having been

justified by his grace, we might become heirs in keeping with the hope of eternal life. (Titus 3:4-7)

All Christians must face the fact that they still have a sinful nature clinging to them. Our sinful nature has not changed. According to our sinful nature, we are still vile, lazy, drunken, contentious bullies. In heaven our sinful nature will be gone. But on this side of heaven, we cannot expect to be rid of it.

But when we came to faith in Christ our Savior—when God called us to repent of our sins, revealed his loving heart to us, and brought us to faith in his Son—we became so much more than we were before. When you experienced God's love, peace, and forgiveness, it became natural for you to follow Jesus' commands. God made you a new creation. That's the real *you*.

God "wants all people to be saved and to come to the knowledge of the truth" (1 Timothy 2:4). He reaches out to the godless ones, the rebellious ones, the lust-filled ones, the hate-filled ones, and he saves us "through the washing of rebirth and the renewal by the Holy Spirit" (Titus 3:5).

I was sitting in a state prison yard in the warm California sun. I was waiting for a Christian man, who came up wearing an orange prison jumpsuit. We sat at a picnic table and talked. I asked him how many sinners were sitting at this table. From the pained look in his eyes, I think that he thought I was trying to get him to confess his sin (which he already had). So he was more than a little surprised when I told him that the correct answer was two, him and me.

And the same number of people sitting at that table were enjoying God's mercy. We both had come to faith in Christ our Savior. We both had been washed clean by Baptism. We both will stand with Jesus in glory. ✎

Repent and be baptized, every one of you, in the name of Jesus Christ for the forgiveness of your sins, and you will receive the gift of the Holy Spirit. (Acts 2:38)

17

In Love God Gave
the Gift of Baptism

God revealed his love for the world by giving his people the gift of Baptism.

Baptism is a rather simple act. Let's look at the basics.

Jesus gave us the gift of Baptism when he commanded his disciples to "go and gather disciples from all nations by baptizing them in the name of the Father and of the Son and of the Holy Spirit, and by teaching them to keep all the instructions I have given you" (Matthew 28:19,20). Jesus promised that by baptizing and teaching people, his disciples would bring more people to faith and make more disciples of the Savior. Jesus' disciples were to teach people about the guilt of their sin and God's forgiveness in Christ. Then they were to baptize those who came to faith in him.

The idea of baptism was nothing new to Jesus' disciples. They were familiar with the water washings God had commanded his Old Testament people to perform. If the people of Israel were to be God's people, they and everything they owned had to be pure and clean because that's what God was like. For example,

IN LOVE GOD GAVE THE GIFT OF BAPTISM

the priests had to wash various objects in the temple and the surrounding courtyard. In fact, God had the Israelites include a huge brass "sea" filled with water as one of the temple furnishings so the priests had a ready supply of water. And by Jesus' day, the Jewish teachers had added additional laws for cleansing. The people had to ceremonially wash their pots, pans, couches, and tables before using them for meals.

In Jesus' day, God told John the Baptist to wash the people who came to him. When people repented of their sin, John washed their sins away in the Jordan River. John used baptism to get the people's hearts ready for the coming of the Savior.

So when Jesus told his disciples to make more disciples by teaching and baptizing, they immediately knew what to do.

The ceremony is simple and so are the words Jesus commanded us to use. We are to baptize "in the name of the Father and of the Son and of the Holy Spirit." In Baptism God joins a person to himself. Note that there is just one name. That name belongs to the Father. That name belongs to the Son. That name belongs to the Holy Spirit. Through Baptism the loving heart of God—Father, Son, and Spirit—connects us to each member of the triune God.

Baptism belongs to God, and he has given it to the church to be used according to his wishes. Too often people want to take ownership of Baptism and use it as they wish. And in the process, they change it from a way God reveals his love to us into something about which to speculate and argue.

In my ministry I've seen this happen many times. Let me point out what happens so you don't get trapped and rob God of the glory he deserves for giving us this gift.

Who will be the godparents? This question comes up often. Most Christian families decide long before the child is born and use a good measure of patience and tact if people's feelings might get hurt for not being asked. If some of the potential godparents attend churches not in our fellowship, conflict can arise over what role they are going to play. Timing for the baptism is often an issue: When will the baby be baptized? Should we wait until certain people can fit it into their schedules?

Members of Baptist and other Evangelical or Reformed churches believe that getting baptized is between the child and God. Therefore, the child must be old enough to make a decision to believe and be baptized.

Some relatives demand that the child be baptized in a certain church following certain customs they have used in the past. Baptism becomes little more than an expression of the family's culture and background. Family members want things done their way and sometimes make compromises: "Let's start a new tradition: have the baptism at a new church or performed by a neutral pastor." But again, Baptism is God's gift to us, not a matter of culture or something to be argued about.

Nor does a baptism belong to the person who performs it. That person has not been given the right to dictate the who, how, when, where, and why of Baptism. And what if the pastor is secretly a wicked person or even an unbeliever? Does that invalidate a baptism that person performed? The early church struggled with this problem. Some church leaders caved in the face of persecution and denied the faith. Did that invalidate the baptisms they performed? All of this led to a great deal of uncertainty about Baptism itself.

All of this must be avoided. This uncertainty can turn us away from the heart of Baptism—God's gift of forgiving love in Christ. It can create dissension among family members. It can invite speculation about Baptism based on human reason and cast doubt on the power of Baptism itself. It can lead people away from the fact that Baptism removes strings and conditions. Baptism is purely a gift from the Lord who loves us. ☿

See the kind of love the Father has given us
that we should be called children of God,
and that is what we are! (1 John 3:1)

18

In Love God Joined You to Himself in Baptism

I want my car to start, but I also want it to keep going. Many people are certain about Baptism at the start of a person's life of faith. They believe that Jesus has commanded us to "baptize all nations." They go to special lengths to make a baptism happen. They have a big celebration when it does. But it is much less clear in their minds about what happens afterward. What does Baptism do on the day after a person is baptized? Will it keep on working throughout that person's life?

The key is connection. Unless my house is properly connected to the power grid, bad things start happening. Lights go out. The screen on your computer goes black and the data disappears. Clocks start blinking. Heaters and refrigerators stop working.

By nature, none of us were connected to our Creator. We were like the Gentiles to whom Paul wrote. They were "separated from Christ, excluded from the citizenship of Israel, and foreigners to the covenants of the promise . . . without hope and without God in the world" (Ephesians 2:12). But God displayed his loving heart by connecting us to Jesus. Jesus is called Immanuel, "God with us." God created this connection by being made like us in every way. God created this connection by living and dying in our place. He overcame death for us, rose in victory, and now rules over everything for our benefit. By being connected with Jesus, we receive the benefits of his life, death, resurrection, and ascension. Paul continued, "Now in Christ Jesus, you who once were far away have been brought near by the blood of Christ" (Ephesians 2:13).

Baptism is at the center of our connection with Christ. Baptism connects us with what he did for us. St. Paul selects three events from Jesus' life and shows how our baptism connected us with Christ in each of these events. He wrote:

> We died to sin. How can we go on living in it any longer? Or do you not know that all of us who were baptized into Christ Jesus were baptized into his death? We were therefore buried with him by this baptism into his death, so that just as he was raised from the dead through the glory of the Father, we too would also walk in a new life. For if we have been united with him in the likeness of his death, we will certainly also be united with him in the likeness of his resurrection. (Romans 6:2-5)

When we were baptized, we died with Christ. When Jesus offered his body and blood, he covered our sin and paid the debt (the burden of guilt) we owed to God. In a single act he removed from all people the guilt of all their rebellion and all their sins for all time.

When we were baptized, we died with Christ and received the benefit of his payment for sin. Our guilt and shame were covered by his guilt and shame. And when we were baptized, God connected us with Christ as he was doing something for us that we could never have done for ourselves.

Not only did we die with Christ, but we were also buried with him in the water of Baptism. Imagine taking a large-sized garbage scow, filling it with all of your sins, and then sinking it in the deepest ocean trench. It's there for good. Criminals try to bury the evidence, but we don't have to. Our crimes were buried in Jesus' tomb. They are gone forever. They can never resurface and force us to stand before the Judge.

Jesus then rose from the dead. He no longer carried the sin of the world. All sin had been covered by his blood. He rose in glory to live a new and different life. And because we were joined with him in death, we are now joined with him in his resurrection. Right now we are joined with him spiritually; someday we will inherit a glorified body like his.

When did this all start? It started when we were baptized into Christ's death and burial and were given a new life by being connected to his resurrection. Paul explains how our new life in Christ is the foundation for living a life in service to God:

> We know that since Christ has been raised from the dead, he will never die again. Death no longer has control over him. For the death he died, he died to sin once and for all, but the life he lives, he lives to God. In the same way also consider yourselves dead to sin, but alive to God in Christ Jesus.
>
> Therefore, do not let sin reign in your mortal body so that you obey its desires. Do not offer the members of your body to sin as tools of unrighteousness. Instead, offer yourselves to God as those who are alive from the dead. (Romans 6:9-13)

Christ reversed the power sin has in your day-to-day life. Now day after day, by the spiritual power that comes from your baptism, you drown, bury, crucify, take off, and remove the old you. You rise to live for him.

Because Baptism joins us with Christ, we no longer try to find the power in ourselves to serve God (as if by nature we had any). Rather, "I am baptized" becomes our battle cry against the devil who wants to destroy our faith. "I am baptized" becomes our battle cry against the world that wants to make us give up in the face of false teachings and persecution. "I am baptized" becomes our battle cry against the sins we commit every day.

"I am baptized!" What a wonderful gift of God from his loving heart! Q

> *Since we died with Christ, we believe that we*
> *will also live with him.* (Romans 6:8)

19

In Love God Gives Children the Blessing of Baptism

Should I baptize my child? That's a good question. We'll answer that question at the close of this chapter. But before we do that, let's look a little more at the gifts God gives us in Baptism.

Paul writes, "No one can say, 'Jesus is Lord,' except by the Holy Spirit" (1 Corinthians 12:3). The Holy Spirit is the person of the Holy Trinity responsible for taking what is Christ's and making it ours.

In Baptism we receive the gift of the Holy Spirit, and along with him we receive the forgiveness of sin. Ten days after Jesus ascended into heaven, Peter preached a sermon on the Day of Pentecost. Many to whom he preached had been directly responsible for putting Jesus on the cross. He said, "Let all the house of Israel know for certain that God has made this Jesus, whom you crucified, both Lord and Christ" (Acts 2:36).

The people saw their deadly sin for what it was. They were horrified that they had murdered the Lord's Christ, and they felt the force of God's wrath. "Now when the people heard this, they were cut to the heart and said to Peter and the other apostles, 'Gentlemen, brothers, what should we do?'" (Acts 2:37).

Peter told them what to do: "Repent and be baptized, every one of you, in the name of Jesus Christ for the forgiveness of your sins, and you will receive the gift of the Holy Spirit. For the promise is for you and for your children and for all who are far away, as many as the Lord our God will call" (Acts 2:38,39). They were to repent of their sins and be baptized in Jesus' name. They would be forgiven and receive the gift of the Holy Spirit.

Let's start a list: When the people on Pentecost repented of their sins, they were invited to be baptized into Christ, and at that point they received "the forgiveness of sins" and "the gift of the Holy Spirit."

In writing to his fellow worker Titus, Paul reminded the Christians in the congregations on the island of Crete how sinfully wretched they had been before God found them. Paul also reminded them of how God brought them into his family:

When the kindness and love of God our Savior toward mankind appeared, he saved us—not by righteous works that we did ourselves, but because of his mercy. He saved us through the washing of rebirth and the renewal by the Holy Spirit, whom he poured out on us abundantly through Jesus Christ our Savior, so that, having been justified by his grace, we might become heirs in keeping with the hope of eternal life. (Titus 3:4-7)

Rebirth—being born again—is one of several ways in which the Bible describes when a person goes from the darkness of unbelief into the light of faith. St. Paul calls Baptism "the washing of rebirth and the renewal by the Holy Spirit." So we can add rebirth to our list of the blessings that come with Baptism.

Paul used yet another picture to illustrate the blessings of Baptism, this time with something we do every day: "You are all sons of God through faith in Christ Jesus. Indeed, as many of you as were baptized into Christ have been clothed with Christ" (Galatians 3:26,27).

Baptism is not something a Christian does and that's it. It is something we do once, but its benefits continue. It's like putting on a shirt in the morning. You put it on (a onetime act), but it keeps you covered all day long. In Baptism we have been clothed with Christ. God wrapped Christ around us, covering our shame with his perfection. That's the ongoing effect of Baptism. Has anyone ever told you to "remember" your baptism? You were being urged to remember the day when you put on the clothing of Christ that you are still wearing.

Here's a picture my dad taught me. Baptism is like a shower that is always running. You cannot turn it off. As soon as a person enters the shower, all the mud from his or her sinful life is immediately washed off. Sadly, we have a sinful nature and keep on sinning. We keep putting mud on ourselves, but the shower keeps washing it off. None of it sticks.

Our list is growing. We can add being clothed with Christ to our list of the blessings of Baptism.

The apostle Peter spoke about the saving power of Baptism. After Jesus rose from the dead, he went into hell to proclaim his victory to people who rejected him in the past. He mentions the people (the disobedient "spirits") who refused to repent even as they watched Noah build an ark that would save Noah and his family from destruction. Peter wove the saving power of Baptism into his teaching of the salvation Christians have in Christ:

> These spirits disobeyed long ago, when God's patience was waiting in the days of Noah while the ark was being built. In this ark a few, that is, eight souls, were saved by water. And corresponding to that, baptism now saves you—not the removal of dirt from the body but the guarantee of a good conscience before God through the resurrection of Jesus Christ. (1 Peter 3:20,21)

Just as the water buoyed Noah and his family above the destruction of the world below them, so Baptism buoys us above God's wrath over sin and the final destruction of the world on judgment day. Indeed, Baptism saves us. How? By giving us a good conscience before God—a conscience set at peace because Jesus defeated our sin and proved his victory by rising from the dead.

We can add yet another blessing to our list: Baptism saves us by joining us to Christ.

God could have saved us without Baptism, merely through the preaching of the gospel. But in love God gave us something visible, a rite in which our sins are washed away with water. The water of Baptism, however, is connected with God's Word. In the passage below Paul calls it "the washing of water in connection with the Word."

> Christ loved the church and gave himself up for her to make her holy, by cleansing her with the washing of water in connection with the Word. He did this so that he could present her to himself as a glorious church, having no stain or wrinkle or any such thing, but so that she would be holy and blameless. (Ephesians 5:25-27)

Through Baptism and the Word (I baptize you "in the name of the Father and of the Son and of the Holy Spirit" [Matthew 28:19]), Christ cleansed his church and made it holy.

The whole list of the blessings of Baptism looks like this: Baptism bestowed on us the forgiveness of sins, the gift of the Holy Spirit. It gives us new birth. It clothes us with Christ, and in this way it saves us. It cleanses us and makes us holy. It has power because it is connected with God's Word.

What a display of God's love! Truly, God's loving heart is on display in the Sacrament of Baptism!

Let's return to the question we asked at the beginning. Should I baptize my baby? The answer is simple. Is my baby sinful? Does Baptism contain the power of the Word and Spirit? The answer to both questions is yes. Scripture never forbids Christians to baptize their children. In fact, we are told that entire households were baptized at the same time. (For example, see Acts 11:14; 16:15; 16:31-34; 18:8.)

That's our bottom-line answer. Children are sinful, and in love God provided a way by which they can be joined with Christ and have their sins washed away. Q

All authority in heaven and on
earth has been given to me.
Therefore go and gather disciples from all nations
by baptizing them in the name of the Father
and of the Son and of the Holy Spirit,
and by teaching them to keep all the instructions
I have given you. (Matthew 28:18-20)

20

In Love Jesus Joins Us to Himself in the Lord's Supper

A mother rushes into a burning building and perishes after saving her child. We call her a hero! We never have to wonder if she loved her child; her actions proved it beyond a doubt. A father dives into the icy water to save his child but dies in the process. We call him a hero! We never have to wonder if he loved his child; his actions demonstrated that with absolute certainty.

God's Son rushes into the world to save a world dying in sin. We never have to wonder if God loves us. His actions demonstrate that with absolute certainty.

Police officers say that domestic disputes are some of their most difficult calls: "You step in the middle, and they can both turn against you." Jesus stepped in between the ones who owed full payment for their sins and the One who demands the payment to be made. But this is no marriage dispute. It is the just anger of God against sinners who unjustly argue their case against him.

Jesus stepped into the middle, not as an arbitrator but as a Redeemer. He stepped in to purchase human beings for God by paying the ransom price of a perfect life and an innocent death—things that no human being could ever pay for. His work as Redeemer is the center of Christianity. It is also the center of a special rite he gave the Christian church called Holy Communion. You may have heard it called the Eucharist or the Lord's Supper, but they all refer to the same thing.

As Jesus' life on earth was coming to a close, he celebrated one more Passover meal with his disciples. John reports that "Jesus knew that the time had come for him to leave this world and go to the Father. Having loved his own who were in the world, he now showed them the full extent of his love" (John 13:1 NIV 1984). As Jesus and his disciples ate their last Passover meal together, Jesus did indeed show them the full extent of his love. He gave them and all believers a special meal, the Lord's Supper.

Some call this meal the Eucharist. This name comes from the Greek word that means to "give thanks." At the supper, as Jesus took the bread and wine and gave them to the disciples, he "gave thanks" (Mark 14:23). So do Christians when they join in the Lord's Supper.

Holy Communion is another name. *Communion* means to "share something or have something in common." Here's a negative example. Paul asks, "What partnership does righteousness have with lawlessness? Or what fellowship [communion] does light have with darkness?" (2 Corinthians 6:14). Righteousness and lawlessness, light and darkness have nothing in common.

What happens in Holy Communion, however, is a very positive example. Two things are coming together. They are sharing in something. They have something in common.

Let's look at the different kinds of fellowship that exist in the Lord's Supper.

Paul helps us understand what Jesus is serving at this meal. He wrote, "The cup of blessing that we bless, is it not a communion of the blood of Christ? The bread that we break, is it not a communion of the body of Christ?" (1 Corinthians 10:16).

In the Lord's Supper, the wine is joined with the blood of Christ. The bread is joined with the body of Christ.

Mark does the same when he records what Jesus said when he started Holy Communion. "While they were eating, Jesus took bread. When he had blessed it, he broke it and gave it to them, saying, 'Take it. This is my body'" (Mark 14:22). Then after supper, "he took the cup, gave thanks, and gave it to them. They all drank from it. He said to them, 'This is my blood of the new testament, which is poured out for many'" (Mark 14:23,24).

These special words united the bread with Jesus' body and the wine with Jesus' blood. Jesus connected the bread in his hand with his body that would soon be hung on the cross. He connected the wine in the cup with his blood that would be shed on the cross the next afternoon. And this was more than symbolism. It was creating the most intimate communion possible. The bread *is* his body. The wine *is* his blood.

There is another connection, another communion, in Holy Communion. Jesus connected his body and blood with the person who is eating and drinking them. Jesus wants the one who is eating and drinking to be absolutely sure that the promises he makes in this meal are made to him or her personally. Paul recorded Jesus' words when Jesus gave his disciples his body, "This is my body, *which is for you*" (1 Corinthians 11:24, emphasis added). You can't look at another person and say, "Well, that's fine for you, but he isn't talking to me." Jesus reassures us that his body and blood in the Lord's Supper are specifically for you.

Jesus gave us the Lord's Supper on the night he was betrayed and sentenced to die for us. In the Old Testament, God promised the Israelites that an innocent lamb's blood would save their firstborn from death. (See Exodus 12:1-14 for the details.) Jesus is our Passover Lamb who saves all people from eternal death. When John the Baptist saw Jesus, he said, "Look! The Lamb of God, who takes away the sin of the world!" (John 1:29). The true Passover was at hand. The Lamb would soon give his body and shed his blood to take away the sin of the world. In the

Lord's Supper, Jesus gave us the true Passover Lamb (himself) to eat and drink.

There is one more communion that takes place in the Lord's Supper. It is a wonderful thing to stand side by side and shoulder to shoulder *in communion* with people who partake of Holy Communion as Jesus instituted it. As we eat and drink together, we remember that our Savior's love prompted him to suffer and die in our place. Together we trust that the bread and wine are the body and blood of Christ given and shed for the forgiveness of the world's sin—the forgiveness of *our sin.* ⌒

There is one God and one mediator between
God and mankind, the man Christ Jesus,
who gave himself as a ransom for all. (1 Timothy 2:5,6)

21

God Graciously Connects Us to Jesus' Death

A warning echoed throughout the garden. Adam heard it. So did Eve. "The LORD God gave a command to the man. He said, 'You may freely eat from every tree in the garden, but you shall not eat from the Tree of the Knowledge of Good and Evil, for on the day that you eat from it, you will certainly die'" (Genesis 2:16,17).

The devil assured Eve that the opposite was true. He told her, "You certainly will not die. In fact, God knows that the day you eat from it, your eyes will be opened, and you will be like God, knowing good and evil" (Genesis 3:4,5). Satan promised a fuller life than the one God had given Adam and Eve. They would understand not just good but both good and evil. In a sense Satan was right, but it was a half-truth, a lie. They *had* experienced good in all its perfection. They *would* experience evil in all its perfection. But after they experienced evil, they would *never again* experience the goodness in which God created them. They could never again be good, holy, and perfect in their thoughts, words, and actions like God was.

At that point the process of death began. Adam and Eve died spiritually; they were separated from God, who created them and loved them. Physical death would follow in due course. And if left at that, eternal death in hell would come next.

That, by nature, is what we are all like. That is why physical death haunts us. We hope that somehow God's threat, "You will certainly die," will not happen to us. But we know it will. Death and judgment cannot not be avoided.

One sin breaks a person's relationship with God. Even a single sin deserves an eternity of separation apart from God in hell. We might put it this way: Without Christ, sinners must pay one eternal death in hell for every sinful thought, every sinful word, and every sinful deed they commit. The sinners must also pay one eternal death in hell for every good and loving thought they did not think, every good and loving word they did not say, and every good and loving deed they did not do.

The only possible way out is if someone suffers and dies in my place. But who could that be? Enter my attorney. He sacrificed himself for me. He paid my bill of trillions of deaths and made *atonement* for me. (*Atonement* is a word made up from *at* and *one*.) Jesus' sacrifice of atonement is the payment that takes away my sin and makes me "at one" with God again.

So the whole focus of the Bible is the loving heart of the One who willingly chose to die in the place of every man, woman, and child who has ever lived and will ever live. The Bible from beginning to end keeps Jesus' sacrifice in front of me. The Father reveals his love for the whole world in this simple way: "He gave his only-begotten Son, that whoever believes in him shall not perish, but have eternal life" (John 3:16).

On the night he was betrayed, Jesus showed his disciples "the full extent of his love" (John 13:1 NIV 1984). He connected them and us to his death. Each one of us can say, "His death became my death in the same way that his life becomes my life. His resurrection and ascension will become my resurrection and my guarantee of a life with my Father in heaven forever."

Christ established this connection when he drew all people with all their sins to himself on the cross (John 12:32). And he connected me to him when he brought me to faith in this fact. But in love, Jesus goes further. He connects me to his death by giving me his body that hung on the cross and his blood that dripped from his wounds.

He does this in a remarkable way. He connects his body to bread. As I eat the bread, I receive his body. He connects his blood to wine. As I drink the wine, I receive his blood. The Passover Lamb came *for me*.

Sometimes Christians say that we celebrate the Lord's Supper. And the person who leads the service is sometimes called the celebrant. Indeed, coming to the Lord's Supper is a celebration. The death of Jesus (along with his resurrection and ascension into heaven) is the most important thing that ever happened, for it gave me life. In the Lord's Supper, I celebrate the fact that God's love in Christ is *for me*.

On the wall in my daughters' room hangs a picture. On a hill in the background are three empty crosses. A little lamb, symbolizing a child in Christ, looks out of the picture. In big letters in the corner of the picture are the words "FOR ME!"

No wonder believers sometimes walk away from the Communion table filled with awe, overwhelmed by what they have just received. Others walk away with a smile of profound joy on their face. Still others are lost in meditation, impacted by the presence of Jesus himself in the Supper.

The Lord's Supper is no place for frivolity. It is no place for allowing other things to enter our minds. It is no place for those who have no interest in forgiveness. It is no place for people who do not understand that they are eating and drinking Jesus' body and blood. The parts of the worship service before the Communion celebration are designed to focus our attention on our deep need for what we are about to receive. They help us remember Jesus' death and the implications of that death for us. They help us think about why we can truly depart in peace after we have communed.

After Jesus and his disciples had finished the Lord's Supper, they sang a hymn, most likely one of the psalms. We don't know which psalm they sang, but perhaps Jesus chose Psalm 118, which would strengthen the disciples for the coming hours:

The stone the builders rejected has become the cornerstone.
This is from the LORD.
It is marvelous in our eyes.
This is the day the LORD has made.
Let us rejoice and be glad in it. (Psalm 118:22-24)

The leaders among God's Old Testament people, who should have built them up in the faith, would have no love for God's cornerstone. But that cornerstone is the rock on which the church would be built.

That night in the hours of darkness the disciples faced their worst temptation. They all failed. They all sinned. But in the coming days, they would celebrate the power of forgiveness in the Supper Jesus had just given them. The Lord's Supper was for sinners. It was *for them*, and it is *for me*. ◯

You turned my mourning into dancing.
You removed my sackcloth and clothed
me with joy. (Psalm 30:11)

22

The Blessings of Holy Communion Last Forever

An insurance agent met with me in the dorm my freshman year in college. He suggested that I start thinking about retirement! He asked me if I was sure I would save enough to retire comfortably without having to work. He showed me the math! A little money saved regularly each month would accumulate and accrue interest. I would end up with much more than I ever thought.

It is not enough that God the Father loved me once upon a time. I need God's love to last forever. I need God's mercy to endure forever. I need God's promises to be guaranteed. It would be nice to have a down payment from God to assure me that he will do what he has promised.

God has given us all of that. The death of Jesus is a "once for all people for all time" event. Listen to how some of the New Testament writers assure us of that.

Paul explained what Jesus did and applied it to us: "The death he died, he died to sin once and for all, but the life he lives, he lives to God. In the same way also consider yourselves dead to sin, but alive to God in Christ Jesus" (Romans 6:10,11).

Peter put it this way, "Christ also suffered once for sins in our place, the righteous for the unrighteous, to bring you to God" (1 Peter 3:18).

The writer of Hebrews makes the point a number of times. He compares Jesus and the priests who served in the temple at Jerusalem: "Unlike the other high priests, he does not need to offer sacrifices on a daily basis, first for his own sins and then for the sins of the people. In fact, he sacrificed for sins once and for all when he offered himself" (Hebrews 7:27). Jesus does not have to die over and over again. His one payment was enough for all people, for all time, for all sins. In another place the writer described why Jesus could enter heaven and how he paved the path for us to go there too: "He entered once into the Most Holy Place and obtained eternal redemption, not by the blood of goats and calves, but by his own blood" (Hebrews 9:12).

It is profoundly comforting to know how intimately Jesus loves me and knows me. Each time I go to the Lord's Supper, I am connected with his death—the death that paid for the specific sins I have committed.

"You may depart in peace," my pastor says after I have communed, because Christ has once again joined me with himself in a most wonderful way. He wants to maintain that communion between him and me. I know that no matter how often I have sinned, I can find God's loving heart in the Lord's Supper. Every sin and the fear of death, which that sin creates, have once again been removed through the body and blood of Christ, which I have literally taken into myself.

Jesus invites us, "Come to me all you who are weary and burdened, and I will give you rest" (Matthew 11:28). The Savior gives us peace more profound, more restful, and more secure than the best night's sleep we have ever had. His peace is everlasting.

Jesus' words, "for you," supply us with the power and strength that we need to live for him. In a letter Paul wrote to Timothy just before he died, Paul wrote about the power and strength God has given us:

God did not give us a timid spirit, but a spirit of power and love and sound judgment. So do not be ashamed of the testimony about our Lord or of me his prisoner. Instead, join with me in suffering for the gospel while relying on the power of God. He saved us and called us with a holy calling, not because of our works, but because of his own purpose and grace. This grace was given to us in Christ Jesus before time began, and it has now been revealed through the appearance of our Savior Christ Jesus, who abolished death and brought life and immortality to light through the gospel. (2 Timothy 1:7-10)

Freed from guilt and death, we can give the same forgiveness to our enemies, to the people who might never forgive us. We know that his death was also for them!

The Lord's Supper prompts us to take a good hard look at the purpose and mission of our church. Does the forgiveness of sins in Christ, delivered freely and without charge to a fallen world, occupy center stage in our thinking and way of doing things? Will the people who visit our church hear the good news? Will they begin to grasp the length, the height, and the depth of the love of God when they hear the words of the gospel and meet people who reflect God's love? Will they be able to depart in peace because they have heard about the hope they can have through faith in Christ? The Lord will bless our work so that happens each Sunday.

Finally, God has given us a down payment on our future. He has given us the Holy Spirit as a guarantee that we are God's dearly loved children and heirs of heaven.

The Bible writers wrote in words that resound with certainty. These words are far more certain than any chart about future investment returns offered by a financial advisor. The believers of long ago looked for a symbol to remind them of the certainty of their hope in Christ. They used a picture they found in the book of Hebrews: a massive ship's anchor! Watch a video of an aircraft carrier dropping anchor. That ship is not going anywhere. Its anchor is lodged secure. Jesus entered heaven and anchored himself there. He urges us to hold on to him by the rope of faith. We can be confident that heaven's blessings are ours because our anchor, Christ himself, is firmly set. ⟶

We have this hope as an anchor for the soul.
It is sure and firm, and it goes behind the
inner curtain, where Jesus entered ahead of
us on our behalf. (Hebrews 6:19,20)

PART 4

God's Heart

Is On Display in
His Gift
of Prayer

23

God Always Answers
Our Prayers

On the day Adam and Eve sinned, communication between them and God was strained at best. They feared talking to God. They knew what he was going to say. It's not that God didn't want to talk to them, but he couldn't talk with them as he had before. He had to confront their sin.

But our loving God took it on himself to confront their sin. That's what we have been seeing throughout this book. In love, he sent a Savior. In love, he told us about the Savior in his Word. In love, the Holy Spirit went to work through God's Word, convincing us of the horror of our sins and the peace God has restored between him and us. In love, God gave us two sacraments, rites through which he gives us Christ's forgiveness in special ways. In Baptism he washed away our sins. In the Lord's Supper he gives us Christ's body and blood.

You have believed these truths. They have reopened the door of communication between you and God. God shows you the horror of sin, but he does that only so he can show you the depth of Christ's sacrifice for you. You, in turn, can go to him in prayer—for forgiveness and help in every need. And you can speak to him as a child speaks to a loving father.

Let's think about prayer.

There are a lot of human rules about praying: fold your hands, close your eyes, keep your feet still. Pray for at least an hour a day. Pray when you get up in the morning and go to bed at night. Pray before and after meals. There is nothing wrong with those rules, and they can be helpful, but they don't assure us that God will hear and answer our prayers.

What does Scripture tell us? Can we find principles in Scripture that will help us pray to the Lord in a God-pleasing way? Does Scripture assure us that God is listening and will answer our prayers? It does.

Before all else, we must always go to God with Jesus on our minds. When Jesus died, he removed our guilt forever. That means that we can enter the Father's presence without guilt, without sinful failings, without defects, and so without fear. "Christ Jesus, who died and, more than that, was raised to life, is the one who is at God's right hand and who is also interceding for us" (Romans 8:34)! What's more, "God also placed all things under his feet and made him head over everything for the church" (Ephesians 1:22). And that means for you.

In Romans chapter 8, Paul makes more gospel promises about prayer. We might consider our prayers confused and clueless, but to God they are perfect and clear. That's because we have someone living within us who is praying perfect and clear prayers on our behalf. Paul writes:

> The Spirit helps us in our weakness. We do not know what we should pray for, but the Spirit himself intercedes for us with groans that are not expressed in words. And he who searches our hearts knows what the mind of the Spirit is, because the Spirit intercedes for the saints, according to God's will. (Romans 8:26,27)

With those prayers going before God's throne of grace, we can be sure that all things work together for our good.

With that as our foundation, we can look for other instructions Scripture gives us about prayer. It's a surprising list.

The psalmist David wrote, "May the speech from my mouth and the thoughts in my heart be pleasing to you, O LORD, my Rock and my Redeemer" (Psalm 19:14). God hears not only the words we speak but also the thoughts of our minds. And he hears even the desires of our heart. David also wrote, "He opens his hand, and he satisfies the desire of every living thing" (Psalm 145:16).

With this in mind, we can better understand what Paul meant when he told us, "Pray without ceasing" (1 Thessalonians 5:17). Paul does not necessarily have in mind formal prayer—times when we express ourselves in words. Rather, it's always having him in our thoughts and going about our day-to-day work with a desire to live for him and do everything for his glory. It means being filled with a desire for his help in all situations. It's about the kind of prayer we offer to God while cleaning the garage, fixing dinner, or driving to work.

James tells us to pray without any doubt that our prayers will be answered:

> If any one of you lacks wisdom, let him ask God, who gives it to all without reservation and without finding fault, and it will be given to him. But let him ask in faith, without doubting, because the one who doubts is like a wave of the sea, blown and tossed by the wind. In fact, that person should not expect that he will receive anything from the Lord. (James 1:5-7)

Imagine how many prayers are canceled by uncertainty—uncertainty about God's willingness to hear; uncertainty about God's desire or ability to answer; uncertainty about whether a prayer is proper, appropriate, or rightly worded. For those who come to God through the sacrifice of Christ, there can be no doubt. If Christ died for us, then "let us approach the throne of grace with confidence, so that we may receive mercy and find grace to help in time of need" (Hebrews 4:16).

Some express uncertainty like this: I quit praying because God doesn't answer my prayers anyway. I've prayed and prayed, but it doesn't seem to work.

But it is wrong to put a time limit on God. Consider that Abraham prayed for 25 years for the son God had already promised him. Think about the faithful in Israel, who prayed for four hundred years that God would bring them to the Promised Land and for four thousand years that God would send the promised Savior. Jesus said, "I tell you, keep asking, and it will be given to you. Keep seeking, and you will find. Keep knocking, and it will be opened to you" (Luke 11:9).

Jesus also told a story about a man who needed a loaf of bread at midnight for unexpected company. He knocked persistently at the house of his neighbor, who didn't want to help him. However, the neighbor got up and gave him bread in order to stop the pounding.

He told a similar story about a judge who neither cared for God nor people. A widow kept on asking him for justice. He finally resolved her case because he was tired of listening to her. Jesus applied this to the injustices Christians suffer for their faith and concluded, "Listen to what the unjust judge says. Will not God give justice to his chosen ones, who are crying out to him day and night? Will he put off helping them?" (Luke 18:6,7).

So pray with boldness and confidence. Our Father in heaven has commanded you to pray. Our Father in heaven loves and cherishes you as his own dear child. Our Father in heaven will answer your prayers because he has made you his child and heir forever. ∅

The LORD our God is near us whenever we
pray to him. (Deuteronomy 4:7 NIV)

24

What Should We Ask For?

My daughters came to me with a broken toy. "Daddy, Daddy, please fix this!" The toy was a favorite, and I was surprised they weren't sadder. But it's likely they weren't worried. They had no doubt that I could fix it. They were certain I loved them enough that I would stop whatever I was doing and immediately repair the toy.

But I took one look at the broken toy and saw it was beyond repair. I took another look at their hope-filled eyes. I knew I was going to disappoint them.

That scenario is common in our world. Few answers. Many disappointments.

But when it comes to our prayers to God, there are always answers, and they are never disappointing. When the disciples asked Jesus to teach them what to pray for, Jesus gave them a simple prayer. We call that prayer the Lord's Prayer. It contains seven things to pray for, each of which opens up a world of specific prayer requests.

We are not going to examine the Lord's Prayer here. Rather, we'll look at some of the things Paul prayed for. There is a beautiful section from the book of Ephesians in which Paul opens his heart to the Christians in Ephesus and to us. Paul reveals what he prayed for:

> For this reason I kneel before the Father of our Lord Jesus Christ, from whom the entire family in heaven and on earth receives its name. I pray that, according to the riches of his glory, he would strengthen you with power through his Spirit in your inner self, so that Christ may dwell in your hearts through faith. Then, being rooted and grounded in love, I pray that you would be able to comprehend, along with all the saints, how wide and long and high and deep his love is, and that you would be able to know the love of Christ that surpasses knowledge, so that you may be filled to all the fullness of God. Now to him, who is able, according to the power that is at work within us, to do infinitely more than we can ask or imagine, to him be the glory in the church and in Christ Jesus throughout all generations, forever and ever! Amen. (Ephesians 3:14-21)

Paul kneels before the Father. Our Father is the only one who can answer our prayers. He alone possesses the kingdom, the power, and the glory forever.

We can call God *our* Father because through his Son he has created a family in Christ. He has called us into that family; you are his child.

Paul can rest his prayer on God's glory. God's glory is not just his flashing brilliance. His greatest glory is his love for us, his forgiveness in Christ, and his desire that we call him our Father. For this reason, Paul can confidently ask God to send his Holy Spirit to give us power in our "inner self," that is, the new person he has created us to be.

Earlier in Ephesians Paul had prayed that God would give the Ephesians the Holy Spirit. Paul told them, "I keep praying that the God of our Lord Jesus Christ, the glorious Father, will give you the Spirit of wisdom and revelation in knowing Christ fully" (Ephesians 1:17). The Holy Spirit has taken the seed of his

Word—the good news of forgiveness—and by his power he has planted it in our hearts so we believe it. From that beginning the Holy Spirit will give you an ever clearer understanding of the hope you have in Christ.

Paul continued:

I pray that the eyes of your heart may be enlightened, so that you may know the hope to which he has called you, just how rich his glorious inheritance among the saints is, and just how surpassingly great his power is for us who believe. It is as great as the working of his mighty strength, which God worked in Christ when he raised him from the dead and seated him at his right hand in the heavenly places. (Ephesians 1:18-20)

It takes great power to enable naturally blind people to see. That's the kind of power at work in you. That's the kind of power Paul is praying that God would continue to give you.

Let's get back to the prayer we're thinking about. The Holy Spirit rooted and grounded you in God's love in Christ. He did that when he brought you to faith. But it doesn't end there. God wants us and all of his forgiven and holy people to comprehend "how wide and long and high and deep his love is" (Ephesians 3:18). He wants us to get out our tape measures and measure the depth of God's love. He wants us to be surveyors and map out just how far God's love extends. He wants us to be timers so that we can clock just how long God's love will last.

When you do that, you'll discover that God's love for you is deeper than the bottomless trenches of the ocean. God's love for you covers all the areas of your life and all the circumstances of your existence. God's love for you lasts forever.

Paul also prays "that you would be able to know the love of Christ that surpasses knowledge" (Ephesians 3:19). Paul wants you to experience and enjoy God's love in all its vastness. As this happens more and more, you will grow toward the goal of being "filled to all the fullness of God" (Ephesians 3:19).

"Could this ever happen to me?" you ask. Paul answers, "Yes, that and more." God's love and his power at work in us are so immense that he is able "to do infinitely more than we can ask or imagine" (Ephesians 3:20).

God's great love is what makes him glorious. His glory is the fact that he has brought us into his family and fills us with his love. God's glory will be on display in Christ Jesus to the end of time. For this God deserves our worship and praise. He deserves that we all be display cabinets for God's loving heart—forever!

What should you pray for? Your prayers to God can imitate Paul's prayer for you. You can pray that God would reveal the full extent of his love to your fellow Christians. As you do this, you will also be praying the Lord's Prayer. As a result of your prayers, your fellow Christians will be assured that God is their Father, and they'll have confidence in praying to him. Then their hearts will be made holy and set aside for God's use; then his kingdom will more and more come into their hearts; then they will more and more take part in causing his gracious will to be done; then they will have confidence to ask God one day at a time for what they need in life; then as they grow to know Christ more and more, they will want to forgive others as Christ has forgiven them; then they will yearn to flee temptation and avoid Satan's evil desires. Finally, they will experience what all believers know by faith: the kingdom, the power, and glory belong to our God.

The prayer from Ephesians chapter 3, chosen as a model of God-pleasing prayers, is focused on God's love—that we grasp the full extent of God's love and see God's love in action in our lives. What a perfect prayer Paul offered to our God who is love! What a perfect prayer to use as a pattern as we pray for each other. ◯

I pray that you would be able to comprehend,
along with all the saints, how wide and long and
high and deep his love is. (Ephesians 3:18)

Conclusion

Do You Have Any More Questions?

I will never stop asking questions. I want to know and understand what God says to me in his Word.

As a little boy I learned to say the words "What does this mean?" from Martin Luther's Small Catechism. Luther was teaching us to ask questions. Does your time with the Bible sometimes raise more questions than answers? Don't worry. God is using his Word to stir up your heart with curiosity and a hunger to understand it.

I hope that you will keep on asking questions. Perhaps we will have the chance to share our questions and find answers together. Listening to each other's questions and joining together in seeking the truth build a partnership of growth and fellowship in faith. We have a chance to show each other that his mercy endures forever. When we find the answers to our questions from the eyewitness Bible writers, their words create fellowship between God and us. That makes our joy complete. That makes God's joy complete!

What is more, God intentionally puts us in contact with others who are unclear about the basic message of the Bible. They are uncertain about God's love. You and I have the privilege of walking side by side with them. We share with them the sure and certain gospel that reveals the hope God has given us in Christ.

God has surrounded you with fellow believers to help you with your questions. They are parents, pastors, teachers, and many others who speak the truth in love with certainty. So ask questions boldly; search for answers in Scripture.

In this book we have seen that what Jesus did here on earth was done *for us*. John assures us, "This is how we have come to know love: Jesus laid down his life *for us*" (1 John 3:16, emphasis added). Paul comforts us, "He who did not spare his own Son, but gave him up *for us all*—how will he not also graciously give us all things along with him?" (Romans 8:32, emphasis added). Everything Jesus will do in eternity has you in mind. Someday you will hear his invitation: "Come, you who are blessed by my Father, inherit the kingdom prepared *for you* from the foundation of the world" (Matthew 25:34, emphasis added).

God's love sets our hearts at rest in his presence. We have come to faith in our Savior Jesus. He is our brother, and we are now members of God's family. I remember seeing a video of a teenager who had just been adopted into a loving home. As part of her birthday celebration, her parents gave her the adoption papers, signed and sealed. She was speechless and overwhelmed. She could not believe that these people would love her so much that they would make her part of their family, equal to their other children.

God has given us everything we need to know him. He communicates with us through his Word. But his Word is not just a tool of communication. It is also the means by which God gives us his Holy Spirit. The Spirit fills the Word with power that works on us every time we read it and think about what God is telling us there. The Spirit instills faith in our hearts and gives us a deeper and deeper understanding of all God has done for us in love. Since God gave us his Word and Spirit, is there any doubt that he loves us?

God has given us Baptism, through which he gives us the Holy Spirit, washes away our sins, clothes us with Christ, and buoys us above the destruction that will someday come on the world. This too is proof of his love.

God has given us a special meal, which we call the Lord's Supper. In that meal Jesus gives us his body and blood. Think of that! We eat and drink the body and blood of the Son of God. We eat and drink the body and blood of the sacrifice Christ made for our sins. Another proof of his love for us.

God has given us the gift of prayer. Prayer is not one of the ways he comes to us with his grace. It's the way we come to him with our needs and requests. And he tells us that our prayers are powerful and that he will answer them. If God did not love us, would he invite us to come before his throne of grace?

In the previous chapters we examined the blessings God has given us in his love. If you have ever questioned his love, perhaps these chapters have answered your question in the affirmative: "Yes, he does love you. In Christ he is yours and you are his."

But sometimes the problem is not a lack of understanding but a lack of using what we do understand—particularly what we understand about the tools through which God pours his love into our hearts and seals us in his love. I heard of a man who bought a beautiful, multifunction snowblower for Minnesota winters. As soon as it snowed, he woke up early, went out in the cold, grabbed his shovel, and went to work. Did his snowblower work? Of course! Did it do him any good? Sadly, no.

Believers have in their garage powerful tools for knowing and possessing the full range of God's gifts to them in Christ. These tools are powered with the same motor that raised Jesus from the dead. And we believers need that kind of power to raise us from the dead—to sustain our faith and make us more and more like our Father in heaven.

Let me use the last few words of this book to encourage you to get the snowblower out of the garage.

Expose yourself to the power of the Word. Choose a couple times each day to read it. Read books that will help you understand Scripture, but let them be secondary. Read Scripture itself; there is no substitute!

From the beginning, the devil has been pestering humankind, "Did God really say . . . ?" As long as we live in this sinful world, Satan pesters us with that same question. He bombards us with confusing new ideas that twist the truth and repackage old lies. He raises up false teachers who parrot his challenge, "Did God really say?" and then suggest that we answer that question using our own logic and feelings.

When Satan asked Jesus that question, Jesus responded, "It is written." Do the same. Jesus reassures us, "Be courageous! I have overcome the world" (John 16:33). He keeps our minds focused on the loving heart of God, who forgave our sins, adopted us into his family, and gives us every reason to seek his will and follow it.

Remember your baptism, that concrete and vivid way God applied Christ to your life by washing away your sins. Martin Luther said that the most important words he could say were "I am baptized." He took his baptism out of the garage daily and put it to use. He used it to defeat the doubt that Satan put in his mind about whether God loves him. He used it to defeat any challenge that he was saved by faith alone in the cross of Christ.

Never pass up an invitation to the Lord's Supper. Don't leave it in the garage. Make sure you know when your church schedules it. Prepare for the Lord's Supper by acknowledging your sins. When you look at the wafer and the wine in the cup, remind yourself that this is God's love in action, connecting you with the body and blood of Christ that took away your sins.

Finally, don't forget to pray. And don't think you always have to express yourself in just the right words. Live with a mindset of prayer—keeping the Lord in your plans, your ambitions, and your desires. Have a few Christian questions always on your mind with the prayer that God would help you find answers in his Word. Remind yourself that your prayers are powerful and that God—because he loves you—is pleased that you brought your requests to him.

Add all this together and it's clear beyond a doubt: You can be certain that God loves you. Q

I trust in your mercy.
My heart rejoices in your salvation.
I will sing to the Lord
because he has accomplished his
purpose for me. (Psalm 13:5,6)